INTERNAL COMMUNICATIC

A practical guide to
effective employee communications

CW00430362

ABOUT THE AUTHOR

Tony Greener is a partner in Positive Images, a management consultancy specialising in communications, marketing and training. He is the author of a number of business books including *The Secrets of Successful PR* (Heinemann).

Internal Communications

A PRACTICAL GUIDE TO
EFFECTIVE EMPLOYEE COMMUNICATIONS

Tony Greener

BLACKHALL
Publishing

This book was typeset by
Gough Typesetting Services for
Blackhall Publishing
26 Eustace Street
Dublin 2
Ireland

e-mail: blackhall@tinet.ie
www.blackhallpublishing.com

© Tony Greener, 2000

ISBN: 1 901657 47 7

A catalogue record for this book is available from the British Library.
All rights reserved. No part of this publication may be reproduced, stored
in a retrieval system or transmitted in any form or by any means, electronic,
mechanical, photocopying, recording or otherwise, without the prior,
written permission of the publisher.

This book is sold subject to the condition that it shall not, by way of trade
or otherwise, be lent, resold, hired out, or otherwise circulated without the
publisher's prior consent in any form of binding or cover other than that in
which it is published and without a similar condition including this condition being imposed on the subsequent purchaser.

Printed in Ireland by
Colourbooks Ltd

Contents

*To Sue and Clare, my wife and daughter,
in recognition of their patience and understanding.*

Acknowledgements

My thanks are due to all those who co-operated so fully in the preparation of this book and especially to Matt Huber at RMC plc, Kate Hayward at Taylor Woodrow, Rosemary Roberts and Paul Couchman at NWGP, Tony Spalding at Vauxhall Cars, Teresa Ford at BT, Amanda Purkis at Abbey National, Paul Copp at Schering, Ruth Allsopp at Nestlé, Emma Payne at Arthur Andersen and to the late Professor Norman Hart and to Harold Musgrove for awakening my interest in the topic in the first place. I apologise unreservedly to anyone I have overlooked in this paragraph and hope they will remember it is a product of my fallible memory over an extended project rather than an intended slight.

The information contained in this book which refers to specific companies and their internal communications methods was correct at the time of writing. In the relatively fast-moving world of internal communications, however, it is impossible to guarantee complete accuracy, especially in the light of today's rapidly advancing technology.

Tony Greener
October 1999

CHAPTER ONE

Why Communicate with Employees at all?

The Blasted Heath

It was a very dark, wet and wind-blasted night at a particularly rundown part of Birmingham called, appropriately enough, Washwood Heath. It was late in November 1979, and it was getting on for midnight. We were all exhausted after weeks of preparation, writing and rewriting scripts, organising slides, videos and film footage. The unions were being more than usually obstructive, the management was highly nervous, the stakes were quite simply the future of what was then known as British Leyland – now Rover Cars.

Into the entrance of the Drews Lane plant swept a dark green Jaguar carrying the Managing Director. He got out, went into the specially created auditorium in the factory itself, and was faced with over 1,000 employees, most of whom greeted him with jeers, boos and the odd wolf whistle. Not a good start.

He started to address the audience in what was probably the first time a senior manager had embarked upon this type of employee communication exercise in recent years. The reason was the so-called Edwardes Plan, the streamlining strategy that was the only hope if the majority of British Leyland was to be saved in some form from the scrap yard.

The plan had been drawn up in the face of strong political pressure to make Leyland more manageable, more viable and, above all, less embarrassing. The products were at best second rate – the Marina, Maxi, Allegro, Triumph Toledo, 1500 and Dolomite, the Rover SD1, the Jaguar and even the Range Rover, were notoriously unreliable. A market share that had, in 1972, stood at around 45 per cent of the UK market had already been eroded to under 25 per cent.

Nobody really knows exactly how much money the group was losing; interpretations depended upon careful accountancy and political emphasis, but it was certainly well into the hundreds of millions, no matter how it was dressed up. There were, on average, 1.5 industrial disputes every working day somewhere within the group, some led by the notorious works convener at Longbridge, Derek Robinson (better known to the tabloids as Red Robbo). Leyland was then the flagship of British engineering excellence being scrutinised under a very searching political and media spotlight.

The plan recommended shedding tens of thousands of jobs and the total or partial closure of a number of sites. Thirteen locations alone were due to be shut entirely, including the emotive decision to close the MG works at Abingdon, which aroused such fury in the enthusiast and classic car ranks. Predictably – and understandably – the unions were incensed and had called for yet another all-out strike. Full-time officials had persuaded the hot heads to wait for a short time in response to a major new management initiative.

This was to hold an employee ballot, overseen by the Electoral Reform Society, in which all employees – of which there were, at that time, around 120,000 – had the chance to vote for or against the Board's plan. As Sir Michael Edwardes has made clear in his book *Back from the Brink,* if the vote went against the plan, the British Leyland Board would have had no option but to advise the government that the group was unmanageable and that the receivers should be called in. Such a move would have had massive repercussions among the component supply industry as well as the retail trade so that a further million or so jobs were also at stake outside Leyland itself.

In order to ensure that the majority of the employees knew what they were voting for, it was decided to mount a major employee communication campaign, predominantly in the volume cars sector, then called Austin Morris, of which the Managing Director was Harold Musgrove, a tough talking but very human engineer. Perhaps because he came from a Birmingham car working family himself, he seemed to know the mind of the car worker better than most and certainly better than any London-based strategic function could have done.

This communications campaign consisted of Harold touring the major sites – Longbridge, Cowley, Canley, Abingdon, Drews Lane, Common Lane, and a few lesser plants – and presenting the full picture to the employees. Because time was pressing and the jungle telegraph between sites very formidable, the entire exercise was completed in five working days and nights, using both day and night shifts. In all, Harold spoke to about 41,000 employees during this grand tour. He told them the business background, stressing that the competition from Europe and Japan had by now far exceeded British levels of productivity and quality. He sketched in the financial position – which was dire.

He revealed for the first time the new product plan, which provided for a series of new models – the cars that were to become the Ambassador, the Ital, the Metro, the Maestro and the Montego. He showed slides of most of these cars, which had previously been classified information. He even went so far as to show full size clay styling models of the Ambassador, the Ital, the Metro and the Maestro to convince the employees that they really did exist and were actually going to be put into production; much had been promised in the past few years in the way of investment in new product, but very little had been delivered.

Then he outlined what the new models meant to each plant – what would be built where, what levels of staffing (or manning as it was called then) were likely to be needed and, consequently, what kind of future there was for that particular plant and its employees.

But it was the final part of the presentation that was the most courageous and the most telling, Harold spoke for about 25 minutes and then threw open the floor for questions for a further half an hour. There were some hostile questions, some frankly curious ones and some complaining ones, mainly over pay and conditions – although not as many as we had anticipated. I don't remember him ever ducking any; he simply got on with telling the employees what the situation was in clear, simple language that they could understand.

That night at Drews Lane, all this was put into stark perspective by an elderly employee who worked in the tool room, the most militant section of a notoriously militant plant. This tool room engineer didn't have a question; he had a point and it was one which is worth quoting because it is both the starting point and the heart of this book and it answers the question posed in the title of this chapter. "Harold," he said, which was one of the politer ways in which the Managing Director had been addressed that evening, "I've worked here at Drews Lane for 27 years and I've never even seen a director before, let alone had one come down to the shop floor to tell me what's what. I don't really care about this plan of yours, but if you're prepared to come here and tell me about it, I'm prepared to back you. You've got my vote and you've probably got the votes of everybody else here who was wondering whether we still had any management."

The Ballot

Posterity records that, in the employee ballot shortly afterwards, 83 per cent of the employees voted in favour of the plan. Red Robbo was sacked within six months and the long, slow road to some sort of recovery had begun. Arguably it began in Drews Lane that cold, November night when those of us who were there realised with a heart stopping shock why the Group had failed for so long. Was there ever a more tragic example of British management not managing than British Leyland? Possibly British Steel, British Rail and British Coal ran it close, as did the company now known as Peugeot but then known by a variety of owners' names – Rootes, Chrysler, Talbot and so on. Possibly a number of smaller, less well-known manufacturers in the engineering industry, which was at that time undergoing massive change usually involving redundancies. Possibly a few of the more militant areas of the public sector which had been more than usually badly handled, but Leyland did it all in a very public arena, in the early days of the Thatcher administration not noted for either its tolerance to nationalised industry or to industrial unrest.

To cap it all, it wasn't as though a plant like Drews Lane had been wilfully ignored or allowed to run down as part of a tactical ploy. Drews Lane didn't do anything glamorous but made components without which the cars could not be built – mainly axles, steering columns and sub-frames. It had had a resident director for as long as anyone could remember, a series of senior figures, who were supposed to look after the interests of the plant and its employees. Part of this process involved communicating corporate decisions to the workforce as part of a conventional cascade system of internal communications. This could, ironically, have been part of the problem. The site had become, if not a separate empire, at least a principality with a sense of alienation from the centre. It is often a fact that the further away a satellite is geographically from the central policy forming heart of an organisation, the further distanced it becomes ideologically.

This tends to be reflected in a series of tell-tale pointers. For instance, at Drews Lane, there was a time warp of a Directors' dining room complete with all the panoply of Victorian complacency – panelled walls, mahogany sideboard, waitress service, specially reserved places for each director, good quality linen, glassware and cutlery and a choice of menu either free or at highly subsidised prices.

There was, of course, a canteen for the rest of the employees as well, but of a very different type. Set in the middle of a grubby factory rather than in the office block it was marked by Formica tables, rarely cleaned properly, solid, simple food with little or no choice, hard pre-formed plastic chairs that looked permanently grubby and a pervading air of cabbage and cigarette smoke. All this combined to create a wholly different atmosphere from the redolent and misleading prosperity of the Directors' dining room behind its panelled walls.

Naming people blue or white collar workers was still a way of differentiating between hourly paid and salaried staff. In particular, it denoted an attitude, which has now changed (albeit too slowly); an attitude which can only ever be improved by the application of consistent communication principles and practices which create a mutual respect. Unless management respects its employees and vice versa, the chances of pulling together in any organisation are pretty remote. But the attitude of factionalisation, as it was evinced in Drews Lane at the end of the 1970s, was so divisive that any self-respecting internal communications manager might be forgiven for recommending the place be shut down altogether and production transferred somewhere less atavistic.

All this was relatively recent in terms of the development of modern management practices. Similar attitudes exist today in some organisations – although the trappings may have changed so that now everyone eats from Formica tables in uncomfortable plastic chairs – but there are still sections of restaurants reserved for certain sections of management where the chairs are better and the potted palms are watered. More importantly, the divide which is represented by this physical differentiation is often manifested in the way in which management communicates – or doesn't – to the rest of the employees. Very often, it is simply a case of maintaining a company newspaper or magazine, which is probably read by very few employees and understood by even fewer. Management then believes it has communicated, successfully and professionally.

The term 'industrial democracy' was being bandied about by those in the relative forefront of management thinking in the late-1970s – but it clearly hadn't reached Drews Lane, or a great many other parts of Birmingham either, judging by the industrial unrest prevalent in the early-1980s. Not until the end of the miners' strike in 1985, the relatively wider affluence of the mid and late-1980s, and then the ensuing high unemployment levels of the early-1990s was the industrial unrest quelled, and then for the wrong reasons. Moreover, who is to say it has gone away? Every week media reports rumblings, threats of strikes and other industrial action, although the efforts are more sporadic, less organised and less entrenched than the highly orchestrated unrest of the 1970s and early-1980s.

As an enlightened society, the UK, and particularly its larger organisations, has come some way since the 1970s – but not so very far. A survey at Salford University published in May 1996 reported that British managers rated their own internal communications effectiveness as a dismal 5.6 out of 10. And, although 90 per cent of large companies now use e-mail, 60 per cent use videos and 40 per cent business television, two-thirds of all employees don't believe the content of the messages, according to the same survey. In fact, over half (55 per cent) say that the channels of communication have worsened, not improved; and this is the caring 1990s.

So, what has happened to the industrial democracy with which we set out so blithely and confidently in the early-1980s? Is the concept still alive or have years of substantial unemployment blunted the necessity for communicating with a workforce which can usually be replaced relatively quickly and inexpensively? Has the attraction of investment from overseas, especially from nations such as Japan and the US where, arguably, less emphasis is placed on the need to communicate openly with employees, actually put the trend of open communication into reverse gear?

This book will try to answer some of these questions, at least in part. In the process it will take a look at some of the best – and worst – practices currently available and try to point out some key issues for managers to consider. Some issues will not be new; a few may be too new to gain instant approval, but all will at least try to tackle an issue which has not been widely addressed in management books in recent years: do organisations in the UK and elsewhere communicate properly with their employees? If they do, what are the lessons to be drawn for others? If they don't, what can they do to improve matters?

Does it Matter?

There is a very fundamental question to address first. Is internal communications really important anyway? Does it matter if employees are not kept informed of every last aspect of an organisation's activities and neuroses?

The answers to these questions depend, to a certain extent, on what sort of organisation is being considered and what it is trying to achieve. If it has any pretensions at all about serving a customer base, about operating in a competitive environment, about offering a service to the general public, then it is vital that it pays full attention to the question of internal communication. If it does not, it generates the proverbial mushrooms – employees who are kept in the dark and fed on manure.

Such employees will not try their hardest for that organisation, will not carry out tasks willingly, will not put themselves out for the sake of the customer. We can all think of examples, many of them in the public and service sectors because those are the areas to which we, as consumers, are most often exposed, and most of them are memorable by their awfulness rather than by their helpfulness.

In essence, the importance of internal communication is to create and sustain a commitment among employees, which will help the organisation to achieve its prime goals. That is why it is so critical to the continued existence of any structured organisation, irrespective of what it is or what it does. Too much energy is wasted in internal strife in too many organisations, playing petty politics, arguing over who should do what while nobody does it properly and vying and jockeying for position in a way that makes Nero look positively enlightened. There are no barriers to this type of behaviour – public, private sector, charities, voluntary groups and vast behemoths alike can all suffer from it. The only rule is that the bigger the organisation, the greater the scope for inefficiency by muddled, ill-conceived or amateurish internal communications.

Behaviour patterns also play a major part. It is always easier not to communicate with staff than to communicate with them. What could be easier than doing or saying nothing? There are also cases of staff at all levels being afraid to communicate with others, not necessarily just those who report to them. This is based on the belief that knowledge is power and that as soon as this knowledge has been shared, that personal power base is eroded. Unfortunately, too many organisations encourage this type of thinking with fairly primitive cultures and promotional systems that take too little account of the balance between personal ambition and corporate benefit. The NIH factor – Not Invented Here – has probably done more damage to British industry than most other negative factors put together. By definition, it is based on self-interest, fear, jealousy and insecurity – all qualities which good, professional internal communication should be able to limit to some extent.

Attitudes

At the bottom of it all is the question of attitude and the way in which employees of all kinds are managed and motivated. Since it is difficult either to manage or motivate properly unless there is a reasonable level of communication, that is the starting point for many debates on enhancing commitment.

This question of attitude is a very common result of inadequate employee communication. At its crassest, it was expressed by a rail operating company manager who, when informed that none of the rail operating companies in the south east were listed in any phone book replied "Yes, I know. Nobody knows what to call us; or if they do, they're not telling us, which is more likely. We don't get to hear anything important like that." And this was a middle manager in 1995, not a British Leyland toolmaker in 1975.

In order to generate commitment from employees, the elements of confidence and trust have to be present to some degree first. This often boils down to the ownership and productivity matrix. If employees share the ownership of an organisation and its aims, vision, mission statements and other manifestations of intent, then they will usually try harder to achieve those aims. If there is no shared ownership, the productivity levels can often be very much lower.

This may sound obvious but it is amazing how many organisations tend to ignore it altogether or else to pay it only lip service. Tokenism in internal communications must easily be as rampant as in equal opportunities, racial equality and employing the disabled, if not more so.

For instance, one internal communications audit carried out recently for an engineering company manufacturing small industrial components and turning over around £20 million a year, revealed one or two issues that needed to be resolved. Notable among these was the fact that many of the employees did not know to whom they reported. This fact could be construed as being an impediment to efficient management by many managers, but not by the management of this company. They took the view that employees did not need to know to whom they reported. All they had to do was to carry out the job for which they were paid, and that attitude was held in good faith, not cynically, by a highly paid, highly successful Managing Director who prided himself on his managerial skills.

But doing what you are told to do can be difficult if you don't know what to do, how, when or where to do it or, particularly, why the job is necessary in the first place. Yet this company prides itself on its ability to generate growth and profits; it is also highly typical of many organisations, including those in the public and service sectors, which often regard their prime responsibility as being financial growth or providing a quality service without realising that without the commitment of their employees, they are not likely to achieve anything approaching their potential. True partnership of interests is the only sensible way forward for an organisation that genuinely seeks to achieve a greater target than mere survival.

The Global Threat

Concentrating on the private sector for a moment, this need to encourage employee communication is by no means new – ICI, for example, was successfully holding employee representative days before the Second World War. It has, however, been given a sharper edge and put into a more significant context over the last fifteen years with the gradual but inexorable decline of British manufacturing industry, and the relentless rise of competition from abroad. Initially, this came from Western Europe and North America, then from Japan and now from the Asian tiger economies, predominantly Singapore, Taiwan, South Korea, Malaysia, India and, increasingly and remorselessly, China.

To be second best in this type of company is no longer good enough. To rely on traditional Commonwealth links is no longer an option for British enterprise; the EU is proving to be, at best an ambivalent blessing with as much, or more, potential for damage as for benefit, and to compete in world markets on price alone is not a viable long-term strategy when labour rates in most of Asia are taken into account. Technical and engineering expertise may still be strong in the UK, but no longer occupy the enviable pioneering position of Victorian days when the Armstrongs of the vigorous British Empire were developing products that the rest of the world wanted to buy but could not make for themselves.

In order to compete fully at international level in the late-1990s and into the next millennium, any organisation has to be that much better than the competition; not necessarily a great deal better – being a little better can be enough. Being better, securing the competitive edge, means that:

(a) there has to be one brilliant individual entrepreneur in charge of an organisation – which is possible but rare; or

(b) the organisation is wisely governed by an intelligent and enlightened oligarchy which moves ahead of rather than with the times – which also happens, but relatively infrequently, mainly because internal politics begin to play a part; or

(c) the organisation has to harness the mind strength of its employee base – which, sadly, is as rare as the other two categories, but which is possible if there is a will to achieve it.

Many organisations attempt to harness this employee power, with varying results. Some do it rather well, and this book will look at some outstanding case studies in organisations such as BT, Abbey National, NatWest Bank and Vauxhall Motors and in the public sector at quango, health trust, county and borough council levels. Some do not manage the task – which is, admittedly, a ticklish one even for those experienced in the art – quite so well, and we will also look at some, necessarily anonymous, examples of organisations which come into this category, such as the industrial components manufacturer already cited.

The public sector increasingly mirrors this type of dichotomy; although lagging in many respects in its willingness and/or ability to embrace truly open management and communication systems. In a realm where security is all, job occupancy, the individual's ambition and the cost-effectiveness of the overall organisation, are often a matter for political whim rather than a goal towards which to strive. Mistrust, fear and suspicion abound and the extent of the commitment to true internal communication is heavily modified. Encouraged by a handful of avaricious and often self-styled consultants, some large local authorities believe they have uncovered a gold mine by discovering the 'team brief' method of internal communication. However, no matter how enthusiastically this is embraced by those who use it, it can very easily be sabotaged by managers who fear its consequences.

One large local authority, for instance, has an important department housed outside the main office block just a few yards away across an internal courtyard in another building. Memos sent from one building to the other commonly take eight days to be received on the other side of the courtyard – and there are many memos in local government. They don't need to take this long, but by doing so, they give managers on both sides of the courtyard the opportunity to consider how to reply, to play a waiting game, to deny knowledge if need be and to generally perpetuate the out-moded internal war games of a wasteful bureaucracy.

Until this approach is conquered by a more enlightened set of managers – for few of the current set is likely to adapt to a more open and communications based management philosophy – there is little hope that internal communication will ever achieve the kind of importance it needs.

Furthermore, the attitude has to be enlightened right at the top if the communications flow is to work properly. Not only that, all managers who need to communicate have to realise the value of doing so. If they don't, they can often impede progress to such a degree that they nullify any worthwhile attempts to bring about meaningful change.

Shared Ownership

What can separate the successful from the not so successful in this quest towards shared ownership of success, growth and security is the need to know and the desire to know. Many employees are quite legitimately and correctly empowered by receiving information from management which they need in order to do their jobs better – quality indices, sales figures, customer satisfaction reports, audit results, financial performance summaries, competitors' actions and so on. Much of this information, however, is useful only to certain types of employee – middle managers, perhaps, or those charged with responsibility for certain areas. Much of it does not touch the normal employee at anything other than a relatively cursory level.

However, there is information about any organisation that is, perhaps, not essential reading but which is highly desirable in terms of securing employee commitment. The effect of competitive action in the marketplace can be related to sales forecasts, financial performance and personal security prospects in a compellingly relevant way. A way which is relevant to every employee who cares about his or her ability to make ends meet at one end of the scale and about the chance of genuine career furtherment at the other.

It is the drive towards this shared ownership of information that we shall be exploring during the course of this book. We will look at the development of modern employee communications over the last fifteen years and the way in which it is playing a more strategic role in enlightened organisations which are consequently reaping some of the benefits. Not all the benefits, because that is a long job, but enough to make most of these organisations realise that they are pursuing something worth pursuing.

- We shall look at the various managerial roles inherent in the process, look at some of the more common reasons for not communicating and at some of the ways around these difficulties.

- We shall look briefly into history to identify successful role models whose approach and methods could be usefully adopted in the 21st century.

- We shall look at what managers and others need to know as part of their professional equipment in order to be able to communicate properly with the employees responsible to them.

- We shall look at some of the different approaches to the art as they are adopted by a number of private and public sector bodies and by the markedly different cultures in South East Asia.

- We shall examine some of the methods by which organisations approach the question of communicating with their employees and, where possible, we shall try to assess their impact.

- We shall look at the various developments of thinking in the field, such as the internal markets concept.

- We shall debate the rightful place of the function in any organisation and try to establish where it should be placed and whose property it is.

- We shall review the new and not so new technology, which widely affects the way in which the messages are disseminated. As a foretaste of what might happen in due course, we shall try to take a glimpse into the future to see what it is that could be done that is not yet being done.

- We shall look at the records of a few of the most successful employee motivators to see what they have or had that modern managers would benefit from and we shall try to work out how far highly efficient communications can support charisma.

Above all, we shall look at the needs of the modern manager and try to ascertain what can be done in most organisations to improve the situation just a little. As de Bono said, it doesn't have to be a major improvement in most cases, just enough to achieve the competitive edge. It should not be that hard. Should it?

In the Beginning

Addressing the Troops

So, how did internal communications start in modern times? How does it interact with various political, economic, social and cultural factors and how has it developed – or not developed – over the years?

It is tempting to trace the history of the practice back to Ancient Greece or the Roman Republic. In those societies, with fewer inhabitants than our present society, communication was easier partly because geographical distances were shorter and more convenient until the later development of the huge Roman Empire.

As with several other institutions – the law, the army, the civil administration, for example – the Romans showed the way for many modern management methods. As early as 350BC, the Republic had a version of a crisis management plan, which involved communicating widely with a large number of key citizens, military units and civil authorities. While it may have stopped short of some of the corporate defence techniques employed today, we can assume that, since it was followed by around 750 years of highly successful Empire-ruling, it worked tolerably well.

The Greek and Roman approaches to internal communications – that is, to those citizens of the City State who wielded political power en masse and on whose trading activities the State relied for much of its mercantile wealth – had one major advantage over many of our modern methods: most of the audiences could not read.

This forced those in authority to go out and communicate openly, verbally, face to face. No hiding behind e-mails, computers, video players or television sets. Simply get out there and face the mob. If you had a good case to present, and if you could speak well, you won them over. If not, you might be torn to pieces, but, at least, it proved your heroism and patriotism and where would classical civilisation be without heroes?

Major commercial operators, of course, did not exist then on the scale of today's global empires and the parallel with modern, internal communication is more profitably expressed in the context of military communications as being the nearest similar situation. Where pay was often poor or non-existent, living conditions either basic or appalling, and job prospects highly uncertain – life expectancy being little more than a few years' service in some cases – there had to be other factors holding together the unity of armies and other military units.

Rhetoric and Leadership

It is no coincidence that the art of rhetoric and persuasive public speaking first surfaces in written records shortly before the birth of Christ. Mark Anthony, who was killed a few years before Christ was born, might not really have said "friends, Romans countrymen, lend me your ears", but he is remembered by contemporary and near contemporary sources as an orator who could sway the mood of the people and a leader who could induce his army to follow him through a trackless desert with very little food or water and precious little certainty of any safety or loot at the end of the trek.

Nor was he alone. Other great generals and statesmen of the early part of classical civilisation must have shared Mark Anthony's way with words to have achieved their feats, to have instilled loyalty and commitment, extra effort and supreme endurance in their forces. Alexander the Great led his army from what is now northern Greece overland all the way to India and never lost a battle. He is still remembered as one of the most brilliant leaders of men of all time.

Hannibal led a rag tag army of assorted north Africans, some leading elephants, from Carthage – now roughly Tunis – up through the Iberian peninsula, through southern France and northern Italy and right over the Alps. He defeated one Roman army and came within a stone's throw of bringing down the might of Rome altogether, before the legions reformed for one final desperate riposte.

We do not have reliable written records of the internal communications approaches of either of these generals, but it is very difficult to imagine them welding together a disparate force of men without having at least some strong communications ability.

Julius Caesar at least left us some of his writings that record a little of what he went through while conquering Spain, France and parts of Germany and England. Interestingly, they also speak of "addresses to the troops" not dissimilar to the words used by, say Montgomery, Eisenhower, Churchill, Hitler or Mussolini from our own recent history. Naturally, the content and context differ, but the psychological approach, the need and determination to carry the enthusiasm of a large force with him through uncertainty, danger, discomfort and a high probability of death or maiming was markedly similar.

But, these leaders all led armies or peoples in times of severe military crisis, which is exactly what modern leaders of organisations do in a different context. They lead groups of employees through a fight for survival, growth, success, recognition, durability and all the other objectives that litter boardroom and governmental conference rooms. Therefore, we will glance at a few examples of military internal communications, especially since they tend to be more graphic and better preserved than their civil equivalents.

The Birth of the Communicator

In the distant times of around 2,000 years ago, we find the seeds of modern internal communications. Leadership – often by example – rhetoric and an ability to command the commitment of forces miles from home and facing a very uncertain campaign have parallels in many modern forms of corporate leadership and management.

Empires in modern times may be more economic than military, but this merely increases the need for commitment and whole-hearted effort from all employees. Strict military discipline is replaced by a new type of social contract which dictates that employees gain rewards in direct proportion to the effort and commitment they put in.

The political philosopher Jean Jacques Rousseau created his famous *Social Contract* in 1762 and in it wrote of a new social contract which bears an uncanny resemblance to some of those encountered today.

> Each of us puts his person and all his power in common under the supreme direction of the general will and, in our corporate capacity, we receive each member as an indivisible part of the whole.
>
> At once, in place of the individual personality of each contracting party, this act of association creates a moral and collective body . . . receiving from this act its unity, its common identity, its life and its will.

Sound familiar? One of the bases of modern democracy and a platform of the way in which private enterprise has sought to work with its employees over the last century or so. The rise and fall of communism over the last 140 years has thrown throw up the question of empirical evidence about Rousseau's beliefs, but it is undeniable that they have played a major part in shaping democratic society which has, in turn, given birth to many organisations which are now examining better ways of achieving an amicable social contract with their employees, without recourse to force, bribery, threats, the law, anarchy or any other uncontrollable force. Even the relatively new movement of 'partnering' has a great deal of basis in Rousseau's original contract; nothing is now an individual's fault but a collective responsibility which replaces that of the individual. It is a seductive, if not yet perfect, alternative to conventional contractual relationships and it may form the norm for future employee relationships as well.

> "Under a perfect constitution," Rousseau continued, "the particular wills of all the various individual men would be entirely subordinate and vanish, and the private will of the government would be very much subordinate."[1]

---

1. Jean-Jacques Rousseau, *The Social Contract* (Pelican: 1962) p. 41.

This applies equally well to any such group, such as a trust or trade union, which is a lesser group within the state. Rousseau has the government in mind because in his day it was the most powerful minority group and, therefore, the chief offender by setting up its own private interests in opposition to the general interest. It is, of course, inconceivable that that should happen today in a fully democratic society. Isn't it?

If anything, Rousseau also shows that there is nothing very new in internal communications. Share option schemes, bonus payments, incremental rises, commission on sales or increased customer satisfaction are simply the modern day equivalents of the ancient military practices of sharing the booty and spoils at the end of a campaign, sacking a fallen city or robbing an enemy baggage train.

Uncanny Parallels

Even relatively modern administrative empires have had their internal communications parallels with classical civilisation. Long and vulnerable lines of communication, for example, have contributed to the decline of most of the more modern sea-borne empires – chronologically, those of Portugal, Spain, Holland and Britain. Take, for instance the communications difficulties faced by one of the ablest naval administrators ever, Samuel Pepys in 1666 when England was at war simultaneously with both Holland and France. The naval action was taking place in the English Channel, but the lines of communication seem to have been chaotic to a degree that would be familiar to many modern day internal communications managers when first they assumed their roles.

> Various rumours, true and false, came to the coast from London – how (Prince) Rupert had been sighted off Dover seeking the enemy, how three Dutch ships had been seen in flames . . . and how Sir John Harman . . . had been surrounded by a Dutch squadron and had only extricated himself with incredible gallantry.
>
> On Monday June 4, the first fugitives arrived from the fleet ... fresh from Harwich . . . to tell him that Rupert had joined with Albermarle . . . Two days after came further news, alas false. For some hours all the bells of London rang for a great victory – half the Dutch fleet destroyed, the rest in flight . . . But next day the sad truth followed, that after a four day battle we are beaten . . . lost many ships and good commanders; have not taken one ship of the enemy's . . . Albermarle . . . had half-shattered England's fleet, losing twenty ships and 8,000 men in his attempt to show the superior virtues of military courage.[2]

2. Sir Arthur Bryant, *Samuel Pepys: the Man in the Making* (Collins: 1947) pp. 291–293.

It must have been difficult to organise the tolling of bells for a major naval defeat – and an unnecessary one at that – when only a few hours earlier they had been ringing out for a major victory; somewhat akin to preparing employees for a takeover only to find that you yourself are in the throes of being taken over.

Similarly, modern economic or administrative empires suffer still from a lack of efficient communications, although developments, such as the Internet and e-mail, are improving that situation. Even the marvels of modern technology need human willpower behind them to make them work. It all still starts from the top; if the chief executive figure is not committed to communicating internally, all the other senior managers face a very difficult task.

The Role of Leaders

Some captains of industry, commerce and finance have had rather different ways of going about communicating than those we find at the turn of the millennium. But, with closer inspection, what they were doing was appropriate to the times, society, culture and expectations of the world in which they lived. Take, for instance, the approach of Lord Hillingdon, the senior partner in William & Glyn's Bank from 1873 to his death in 1898. To read about his approach to communications in banking at the height of the British Empire is to gain a glimpse of a long lost world of Victorian simplicity but dynamism. Educated at Eton and Christ Church College, Oxford, Lord Hillingdon sat as a Conservative MP for 30 years before his elevation to the peerage. His wealth may also help to explain in part his success in terms of internal communications.

> By nature, Lord Hillingdon was extremely generous and as a consequence was greatly liked and respected by the staff of Glyn's whom he regularly invited to cricket festivals at his home at Wildernesse.
>
> At the end of his life, when he was known to be suffering with heart trouble, one of the clerks always walked a few paces behind him to Cannon Street station in case he should be taken ill on the way. *The Times* summed him up . . . 'his unfailing courtesy left a pleasant impression on all who came into contact with him'.[3]

The only mystery about this is why he bothered to get the train at all when he could probably have bought up the entire railway company without noticing that his petty cash levels had fallen. The reference to the unfailing courtesy also gives a clue to secret of good communications: even if there is no re-

---

3. Roger Fulford, *Glyn's 1753–1953* (Macmillan: 1953) p. 219.

spect for your audience, courtesy must always be shown. That is a basic human dignity and one to which too few communicators of all kinds aspire at the end of the 20th century.

Yet it will return in some form and the fact that so many organisations have so much difficulty in communicating with – and therefore handling – their employees properly points to the fact that a rebirth of this type of basic courtesy is long overdue. Victorian magnates did not rely purely on their cash books to buy the good esteem of their employees; indeed, very few of them paid wages which would be regarded as anything other than derisory in our own age.

What, therefore, marks out many of the great leaders of the world's nations is not just their military, administrative or financial and commercial skills, but the enthusiasm with which they attacked the task of informing, empowering and gaining the wholehearted commitment of their followers – in exactly the same way that today's corporate leaders try to do.

Prussians, and later Germans, followed Bismarck partly because they believed he could, and would, unite Germany into a whole nation. In four decades of almost unprecedented success in the 19th century, he did just that. At the same time, his contemporary, Napoleon III of France, presided over the dissolution of an empire, partly because he was unable to persuade his countrymen to follow this example and pull in the same direction.

The climax came in 1870/1 at the Battle of Sedan (so horrifically one-sided that a Belgian observer was moved to found the Red Cross movement on the strength of it) and the subsequent Siege of Paris by the Prussian army. Such solidarity as the French showed was on a small scale – groups of partisans, detached units of citizens or Communards, as the formers of the famous Commune were known. Inevitably, they perished in the face of superior, Prussian organisation – whether in the military, diplomatic, civil administration or even artistic fields.

La Gloire

The great skills of tactics, strategy and surprise of Napoleon (Napoleon III's uncle), would have been nothing without the unquestioning loyalty which saw 600,000 followers pour into Russia as part of his Grande Armee in 1812. Barely 10 per cent of that number returned; the rest were overcome by the Russian winter, disease, famine and cold, more than by the Russian forces. Napoleon himself had retreated on ahead of his army, making sure that he brought back with him all the surviving cases of his favourite wine – Gevrey Chambertin – despite the fact that he is probably the first general in history to have the dubious distinction of losing over half a million men in one campaign.

Yet, Napoleon's popularity was not seriously threatened among the French over the next three years and he assembled on the field of Waterloo his greatest ever army in terms of numbers. The Old Guard was as legendary as the Praetorian or Preobrajensky Guards in its unswerving loyalty to one man. It was, no doubt helped by proclamations, such as the one given below, issued to all the French troops a few days before Waterloo.

> Soldiers, today is the 14th anniversary of [the battles of] Marengo and Friedland, which twice decided the fate of Europe. We were too generous then, as we were too generous after [the battles of] Austerlitz and Wagram. And now, banded together against us, the sovereigns we left on their thrones conspire against the independence and the most sacred rights of France. They have begun by the most iniquitous aggression. Let us march to meet them; are we not the men we were then?[4]

Conveniently, in his last rhetorical question, Napoleon, characteristically Gallic to the last, ignored the fact that many of the victors of the earlier battles mentioned had perished long before Waterloo. A selective recall is sometimes no great disadvantage in internal communications; neither is a healthy disregard for those enemies already beaten – but not until they are and certainly not those still in the field.

Ten years earlier, the British admiral Nelson broke with naval tradition, in terms of internal communications between staff and line officers, but significantly empowered his ships' captains, when:

> . . . the day after *HMS Victory* joined the fleet, Nelson asked half the captains to dine with him, and the day after that the other half. 'What our late chief will think of this I don't know,' Codrington wrote with glee, 'but I well know what the fleet thinks of the difference.' . . . His guests made it plain how glad they were to see him . . . When [he] explained to them 'the Nelson touch', it was like an electric shock. Some shed tears, all approved. It was new, it was singular, it was simple and from admirals downwards it was repeated.[5]

Evidently the example of sharing a new and daring strategy with his officers worked well, as did this early example of team briefing and cascade communications; shortly afterwards, in October 1805, Nelson won the Battle of Trafalgar which effectively settled the question of world sea power for the next century.

---

4. Christopher Hibbert, *Waterloo* (Munton: 1967) p. 137. The full text of Napoleon's proclamation of 14 June 1815 is contained in the Correspondence of Napoleon (Paris 1858–1869) ref. 22,052.
5. David Howarth, *Trafalgar the Nelson Touch* (Collins: 1969) p. 68.

Modern Lessons

The parallel with today's corporate approach to strategy is strong. Managers, once let into the thinking of the CEO, will usually contribute more effectively to refining and subsequently, executing a business strategy. If it is given to them as a fait accompli, there is, understandably, less enthusiasm to embrace the approach. NIH ('Not Invented Here') is a massively negative force in too many organisations, and there is little evidence that it recedes with time. Indeed, it is probable that the reverse is the case as times and organisations become more competitive.

Naval affairs had moved on considerably by the time Lord Louis Mountbatten was First Sea Lord in 1955. His approach to the task of slimming down the Royal Navy to suit a peace-time role is exemplified not just by the clarity of his thought and strategy, but by the pains he took to involve his officers and communicate the eventual plans to the sailors themselves.

> The Navy in 1955 was in a dangerously bloated condition . . . It was time to do some drastic streamlining . . . So I set up . . . the Way Ahead committee with myself in the chair and most of my colleagues on the [Navy] board as members to review the whole situation . . .
>
> In the end, we were able to cut down personnel by about 30,000, uniformed and civilians, and save about £15 million a year without losing a single ship from the sea-going fleet.
>
> I went round all our fleets – home, Mediterranean, Far East, East Indies – tub-thumping and explaining . . . Naval morale, which had been dropping a bit, began to revive.[6]

That word 'explaining' is very apt because that is the process at the heart of true and effective internal communications. The need is often to explain to employees what is happening, why and how it is affecting, or will affect, them. Often nothing more is required; yet, how often is even this relatively simple step overlooked?

The parallel could hardly be closer with the 'downsizing', 'streamlining', 'rightsizing' and 'rationalisation' programmes, which have been designed and put in place by most Western corporations and governments in the last twenty years of the 20th century. Neither could the process of deciding the strategy – gathering the board to develop plans – and then communicating, or selling, the concept to those employees affected. Mountbatten must, by definition, have seen and talked to many of the 30,000 personnel whose jobs

---

6. John Terraine, *The Life and Times of Lord Mountbatten* (Hutchinson: 1968) pp. 174–175.

were to disappear. Yet he records that morale rose. That is evidence of some leader, some inspiration – and maybe, some very generous pay-off terms.

Mountbatten's actions in 1955 bear comparison with Harold Musgrove's Austin Morris communications campaign in 1979 – although the term 'communications campaign' would probably not have occurred to Mountbatten in the relatively sheltered mid-1950s.

Internal Newspapers

During the Second World War, there was a resurgence of interest in internal newspapers. October 1944, for example, saw the appearance of the first *Dunlop Digest* complete with dramatic front cover photo of a tail gunner in his fragile turret in a bomber. Presumably, the success of D-Day four months earlier, and the steady advance of allied forces towards Germany, had persuaded Dunlop's managers that it was time to reflect the likelihood of a return to peace-time activity and to prepare accordingly.

The foreword was written – inevitably – by the Chairman, one George Beharrell. It is redolent of old style company newspapers, some of which have changed little in the intervening half-century.

> Through this first issue of *Dunlop Digest*, I should like to congratulate all divisions upon their individual and collective contribution to the vitally important war work of the company.
>
> During the war, many technical developments have occurred which will, ultimately, be adaptable to the needs of peace. New products have appeared for which new markets will have to be found. The manufacture of some articles has ceased and both production and distribution must be re-established. Old ground will have to be renewed and fresh ground cultivated.
>
> All the work involved cannot be properly performed unless there is a co-ordination of divisional activity which will make the utmost use of our combined strength and knowledge.
>
> The *Dunlop Digest*, if actively supported by officials with information to give or questions to ask, will constitute a useful link between those whose great interest is the present and future achievement of Dunlop.
>
> I welcome the *Dunlop Digest*. I hope that it will successfully fulfil its purpose.[7]

Hardly an inspired last sentence but this is, on the whole, sturdy stuff, as befitted the times, almost echoing the Churchillian phrases which had be-

---

7. *Dunlop Digest* (October 1944).

come so familiar to the British public during the preceding five years. The phrase 'never in the field of human conflict' has passed into history as epitomising Churchill; it is interesting to see it quoted in the context of a communications strategy aimed at bolstering the fragile confidence of the RAF in 1940 (20 August) when the Battle of Britain was at its height.

> The gratitude of every home in our island, in our Empire and indeed throughout the world except in the abodes of the guilty, goes out to the British airmen who, undaunted by odds, unwearied in their constant challenge and mortal danger, are turning the tide of war by their prowess and their devotion. Never in the field of human conflict was so much owed by so many to so few.[8]

If phrases like these sound stilted to modern ears and if they might appear to be an object of mirth, it would be as well to record that, for all its apparent quaintness, the *Dunlop Digest* of this era was actually more advanced than the internal communications systems in place at Dunlop during the time of its takeover by BTR in 1985. Quite simply, at this later date, there were no internal communications systems at all: I should know, I was (briefly) Director of Communications at the time – too briefly to remedy the situation.

One could ask "why not?" with some justification. A branding survey, undertaken by one of Dunlop's nine major advertising agencies only three years earlier, had proved that Dunlop was the second best known brand name in the world, behind Coca-Cola. It takes some believing now and, I have to confess that, as I never managed to track down the document that proved so elusive, I suspected it to be apocryphal. Nevertheless, this contention was the basis of much interesting – if eccentric – marketing activity at the time, none of it assuming that internal communications was in any way relevant to the health and future of the business.

Not until Sir Michael Edwardes assumed the chairmanship of Dunlop did the situation improve, and he had the distinction of being in one of the first employee videos to be made in the UK, setting out the current state of the business and outlining where and why cuts would have to be made and investment prioritised. Looking back on it, it is not a very good video – although that wasn't Sir Michael's fault – but it did at least try to put into some sensible context the pain of redundancy and uncertainty faced by tens of thousands of employees all over the world.

Here again is a parallel with military communication. A captain of a global industry facing financial ruin as opposed to facing hostile forces has to devise an internal communications strategy in a hurry that will work for most of the audiences most of the time. Inevitably, there are going to be gaps, but

---

8. Malcolm Thomson, *Churchill: His Life and Time* (Odhams: 1965) p. 321.

the effort and thought processes have been committed and that is, in itself, often a heartening sign for those audiences, be they troops or rubber plantation workers.

Propaganda

The military comparison also raises another question of when internal communications becomes propaganda. For example the Crown Film Unit produced a series of propaganda films during the Second World War, some of them very good of their genre. There is, for example, *Coastal Command* a dramatised documentary about a Sunderland flying boat on Atlantic patrol duties, for which they commissioned special music from Vaughan Williams. All the actors were real airmen or other Coastal Command staff and, while stilted in parts and not as good at the stiff upper lip stuff as someone like John Mills, they, at least, brought an air of realism and first-hand experience to their roles.

Yet this film is really an exercise in internal – and external – communications. It reassured the outside world – the public – in the UK that their waters were being constantly patrolled and action taken against the enemy on all possible occasions. Almost more importantly, because few people who could read newspapers doubted that fact anyway, it reminded the men and women of Coastal Command that, although the RAF or Royal Navy might be more glamorous with their Spitfires and battleships, Coastal Command had not been forgotten and its own contribution was recognised as an important part in the overall war effort.

In the hands of a German propagandist, such as Goebbels, the result could have been much more heavy handed. Overt patriotism, fanatical demagoguery, marching troops, artificially positioned happy, smiling, Arian children and all the rest of the trappings of the Nazi propaganda machine would, no doubt, have rendered it a highly amusing if sinister work of art to modern minds; but this was the propaganda machine that could, and did, command the German media and populace that the first 1,000 bomber air-raid by the Allies had not taken place the previous night. No German cities were piles of smoking rubble, no casualties had been effected and no substantial damage had been done.

Since the regime controlled all the media through the state, there was no other way of ordinary Germans to find out the truth, unless they were unlucky enough to have witnessed the destruction for themselves. Once this had begun to happen on a larger scale, of course, the propaganda became counter-productive as more and more Germans realised the hollowness and untruths that it was peddling. Since, by then, they were powerless to do anything about it, perhaps it didn't make much difference.

Even today, there are world figures who are maintained in their power by small but fiercely loyal units. Saddam Hussein would hardly have survived the 1991 Gulf War without the fanatical support of the Republican Guards. Other regimes – or dictators – are, or have been, sustained by similarly loyal displays by groups of followers, often small minorities in the population. Sometimes, this is based on tribal or ethnic loyalties, but even those have to be reinforced by the classical qualities of open leadership.

Reward and an interest in self-preservation play an undeniable part in this process, but so does internal communication. Those who believe they have been party to shared information from their leader will usually rise to the occasion and display loyalty above and beyond the bounds of normal duty or even hope of reward. Duty and loyalty are dubious and very subjective qualities in many parts of the world and it has been shown by industrial psychiatrists, that money is a satisfier, not a motivator. Money provides the means to achieve short-term need – shelter, food, clothing – but it does not, by itself, engender commitment, loyalty or even greater effort for the good of the organisation, let alone unswerving loyalty. That quality requires open leadership, honest communication and leading by example, which is the essence of good internal communication in any modern organisation.

Automotive Industry

No look – no matter how perfunctory – at the development of internal communications, especially in the UK, over the last few decades would be complete without reference to the motor industry and the mould-breaking role it played in breaking the power of the trade unions. Chapter 1 set the scene in some detail and will not be repeated here. However, it is interesting to note the scale of the problem. In 1977, 250,000 vehicles were lost through strike action in British Leyland alone. That is almost as many as its successor, the entire Rover Group, builds today. When asked to tackle this issue, the government sponsored Ryder Report made four recommendations, all related to pay bargaining and incentive payments. Nothing was said about internal communications, not even to try to defuse some of the strike action that was endemic.

In his book, *The Future of the UK Motor Industry* published in the thick of the conflict in 1979, Professor Krish Bhaskar devotes less than six pages (out of 472) to the question of industrial relations and virtually none to the issue of communicating with employees. Hardly surprising, then, that not a lot was done about the problem until it was too late to save more than a fraction of what had once been a very major economic contributor to the nation's wealth. There were one or two references in this book to internal issues, however.

> "There can be no doubt," Professor Bhaskar averred, "that boredom on the shop floor has led to inefficient and counter-productive customs and practice . . . There is only one way to achieve an

economic solution to a boring and repetitive process and that is to automate the process and use the labour force profitably in maintaining the equipment and trouble shooting."[9]

So that's all right then. Society simply creates factories staffed by robots and pays out a great deal more unemployment benefit. Which, to a degree, is what has happened over the last two decades. It also shows the unthinking approach that has led to so much strife and disruption in industrial sectors. It is hardly surprising that a frustrated, anxious and angry workforce resorted to one of the only ways it knew to bring attention to its problems. In many other countries, this would have resulted in a revolution; at least in the UK it was limited with relatively little blood shedding.

Revealingly, Bhaskar estimated the necessary level of reduction in the labour force to be of the order of 30-40 per cent. In BL alone at this time, that would have cut something like 84,000 jobs. This excluded all the component suppliers, retail outlets and ancillary jobs that would have been affected. Internal estimates at BL at the time were closer to 250,000 once all these factors had been taken into account.

Of rather more weight and authority is Sir Michael Edwardes' own account of the issue of internal communications. In *Back from the Brink*, he wrote:

> These events (particularly damaging strikes at two major plants) brought home to us the need to set up direct communications between management and the shop floor. There was no other way to win the hearts and minds of the men at all levels. Politically motivated shop stewards could not be relied upon to present a balanced view to employees. They had a vested interest in the outcome, which was independent from and usually in conflict with the interests of the business and its employees.
>
> From that time onwards we made sure that on each occasion when an important issue was at stake, the company view was communicated directly to employees as well as through normal union channels.[10]

Not surprisingly, results followed. Sir Michael cites the case of the toolmakers' strike of April 1979. The pretext was wanting separate wage bargaining for their members who, as skilled workers, should, they felt, be awarded separate treatment from other shop floor workers.

This remarkably elitist, but very typical excuse, led to a strike being called

---

9. Prof. Krish Bhaskar, *The Future of the UK Motor Industry* (Kogan Page: 1979) Chapter 7 *et seq*.
10. Sir Michael Edwardes, *Back from the Brink* (Collins: 1983) pp. 87–88.

for 6 April 1979 when between 3,000 and 4,000 skilled workers stopped work – out of around 8,000 who could have done. In a few days, the strike waned as more toolmakers returned to work and other employees covered for those absent from their tasks. Within two weeks it had crumbled, and BL had not lost a single car as a result. Yet, two years earlier, a similar toolmakers' strike, on similar grounds, had cost BL 50,000 cars.

The difference, in Sir Michael's words, was that:

> . . . before and during the strike 100 senior managers spent considerable time on the shop floor – walking and talking in all 34 factories to explain the company's position; why the demands could not be met and the dangers to the business as a whole if production was disrupted.[11]

It was almost too little too late, and it may seem incredible to enlightened managers a quarter of a century later that the situation had been allowed to fester like this for so long. Yet, that is what happens when organisations stop communicating internally.

The Asian Approach

Other countries do not have quite the same problems – although France has a troubled history of unrest, especially in the public and engineering sectors and even Germany is no longer immune to the problem, judging by recent media reports. It is a pleasant change, though, to work occasionally in different cultures where the concept of a social contract is so much more constructive. Look at the culture in Malaysia, for example:

> Another concept, which is closely related to respect for elders and managers, is loyalty. Managers have a moral obligation to care for their employees in return for loyalty and commitment. Very often employees are considered as members of an extended family and the employer a good parent who will protect them . . . It is likely that an employee, who has a good relationship with his supervisor, will also be loyal to the organisation. As loyalty is highly valued, employers expect their employees to be dedicated to their work and loyal to the organisation.[12]

The climate is well-nigh perfect, too.

---

11. *Ibid.*, p. 90.
12. Asma Abdullah (ed.), *Understanding the Malaysian Workforce* (Malaysian Institute of Management: 1992) p. 12.

Winds of Change

In parallel with all these developments, there has been a very substantial change in public – and, therefore, employee – attitudes towards the provision of information by employers. Over the last twenty years or so there have been radical shifts in expectation among most employees in terms of the way in which they want and expect to be treated.

This change has been fuelled by many different factors – political changes, for example, which have put the onus more firmly on employee participation in an organisation's growth and success, be it in public or private sector. Hand in hand with this is the privatisation of many monoliths during the 1980s, changes which have brought about a revolution of attitude as well as huge streamlining in many organisations.

At the same time, the type of work has changed markedly, especially in the UK and Western Europe. No longer is the economy based on manufactured exports; the traditional hothouses of industrial unrest, such as engineering, shipbuilding and mining, have dwindled terminally as the British staple economy has also changed. Even transportation has declined in a massive way; photos of the Pool of London in the 1960s show a River Thames still relatively full of shipping, cranes and wharves lining the banks where now there are either grassy banks or warehouses converted into residential developments.

Newcastle-upon-Tyne can tell a similar story. In the 1960s, the banks of the Tyne used to be lined with Vickers Armstrong engineering shops, one of which stretched for a quarter of a mile. Outside the road was lined with tanks, shells, gun barrels and all the trappings of heavy engineering. As with the Thames, it now leans towards the theme park end of the spectrum; fine for the environment, not so good for employment, export earnings, skills development or a sustainable economy.

The same period has seen the rise of softer industries, largely based on new technology. Computer-related industry has grown dramatically to soak up some of the redundancies left by the demise of manufacturing. In the same time, the role of the employee has changed. Very often, new industries are not unionised, for instance, thereby avoiding some of the difficulties of years of entrenched industrial conflict in traditional manufacturing industry.

Significantly, as this book was being written, the longest running industrial dispute in the UK was finally being settled – a kitchen unit manufacturer who had been on strike for 22 months.

One steel company in South Wales once had a strike lasting 21 months. It was organised and run by a local government councillor who boasted on many public occasions that he had organised the (then) longest running strike in the UK. What happened in the end? The company closed with the loss of over 200 jobs; something of a hollow victory – but perhaps easier to bear if you're a local government councillor in a safe seat.

This change has clearly brought with it a change in attitude. Old employer/employee roles have vanished along with the old order of industry. Blue and white collar workers are terms seldom used today. Far fewer UK employees belong to a union with a political agenda or, indeed, which has much interest in negotiating through other than negotiation methods. Few employees are as hidebound by tradition as their predecessors and many now expect that they will be told what is going on – because they are part of whatever *is* going on.

Modern communications make it very much easier also. Employees have access to fax machines, e-mail, the Internet, intranets, even business television or radio services. No longer do they have to rely on pieces of paper which may, or may not, arrive in time and may, or may not, be understandable.

The Need to Know

This has led to a much greater awareness among employees of the responsibility of managers to communicate as part of managing. It has also led to a higher demand for information of all sorts about the organisation for which they work. It has moved on from a want to know to a need to know and a right to know – the logical conclusion. Managers can no longer rely on a 'trust me I'm the manager' message but are now being faced with a 'tell me because otherwise I can't do my job' message. In some cases, even this is now being replaced partly by a 'show me because that way it becomes much more real' message, which some organisations are finding difficult to put into practice.

Here is a clamour for knowledge and shared reward – often both inextricably linked. Knowledge is no longer confined to the information which helps employees carry out their tasks but, in some enlightened organisations, is now broadened out to encompass more general information. Reward is seen as being no longer the prerogative of the managerial levels – a positively Victorian attitude – but in the shared ownership and responsibility of all – or most – employees for the success or otherwise of the organisation.

This argument, can, of course, be taken too far, but it does have a great deal of currency in the rapidly changing social employment world of the millennium. No longer is the employer/employee relationship about us and them – which, if undesirable was at least clear-cut and relatively simple to handle in communications terms. Waters are now considerably more muddied, lines of demarcation that much less well defined and the whole challenge of internal communications that much more interesting as a result.

One of the more interesting aspects is the timelessness of some of the principles, especially those such as the strength of oral tradition. Considering the relative advantage of Roman leaders whose audiences could barely read, it is interesting to note that times have not changed all that much. In his defining work, *The Uses of Literacy*, published in 1957, Richard Hoggart wrote:

> If we listen to . . . people at work and at home we are likely to be struck first, not so much by the evidence of 50 years of popular papers and cinema, as by the slight effect these things have had upon the common speech by the degree to which people . . . still draw, in speech . . . on oral and local tradition. That tradition is, no doubt, weakening, but if we are to understand the present situation of the working classes we must not pronounce it dead when it still has remarkable life.[13]

A few decades on from that seminal study of British social structure, there may be more reason to question Professor Hoggart's assertions about the lack of effect that media has had on all classes, working or otherwise. Television had not taken off as a really mass medium by 1957 and the video was unknown. Pop culture was to make its mark a decade later and, in theory, bring all the trappings of a liberated and apparently, more literate, society. Nevertheless, there is truth in what he says even half a century later, although the weakening of the tradition has indeed accelerated, probably beyond even his expectations.

It is that growth of new ways of communicating, mass media, multimedia and all the rest of it, harnessing the power of new technology in a way which would have been unthinkable even ten years ago, that we will explore as we go through this book. Yet the principles behind the technology will not be so very different from those of the ancient Greeks or Romans, and would have been recognisable to many of the characters we have briefly remembered from the two millennia since then. Only the trappings and the ability of assisting humanity to communicate have developed.

As Professor Stephen Hawking says, most memorably in a brilliant corporate advertisement for BT dating from 1995:

> For millions of years, mankind lived just like the animals. Then something happened which unleashed the power of our imagination. We learned to talk. We learned to listen. Speech has allowed the communication of ideas enabling human beings to work together. To build the impossible. Mankind's greatest achievements have come about by talking and it's greatest failures by not talking . . . All we have to do is to make sure we keep talking. . .

---

13. Prof. Richard Hoggart, *The Uses of Literacy* (Pelican: 1957) p. 164.

CHAPTER THREE

The Case for Employee Communications

Why do it?

This chapter will look at some of the main reasons behind employee communications policies and will try to establish a common thread. It is based in part on a discussion paper drawn up in 1998 at the request of RMC p.l.c. by whose kind permission it is quoted here. The purpose of the paper was to set out the benefits of employee communications as they are widely perceived by a number of disparate organisations. In the context in which it was created, it drew only on evident need and did not attempt to outline best practice.

Consequently, it has been modified here and extended to take into account a number of other organisations whose employee communications needs are the subject of policy documents, including Schering Health Care, The Body Shop, Coopers & Lybrand and the Corporation of London. It also takes a more global look at the main issues than was absolutely necessary for the original paper, although in RMC a fair proportion of the employees were also based outside the UK (12,000 out of 35,000). There is, therefore, an international aspect to the disciplines of internal communications that will recur as a main theme during the rest of the book.

RMC

A number of senior executives in RMC were not convinced of the need to sharpen up their internal communications. More importantly, they had no one to tell them why it was necessary and what they ought to do about it until late in 1997 after they had appointed a Head of Corporate Communications. This was something of a departure since they had never had such a position before and, although some of his responsibility was, of necessity, concentrated in areas such as media relations and parliamentary lobbying, one clearly identified priority was to tackle the perceived lack of internal communications.

Here is a case of enlightened senior management not prepared to rely on the traditional basket of devices such as the internal newspaper, a document which the new RMC Head of Corporate Communications described as "grisly", but to go out and recruit specialist expertise to fulfil a challenging task.

Yet, in order to convince those senior managers who were sceptical of the benefits of internal communications, and who were described as 'dinosaurs' by some of their colleagues, there had to be arguments stronger than simply quoting best practice. They had to be stronger than simply saying that other organisations did it, therefore it must be a good idea. There had to be some kind of demonstrable benefit to the bottom line, to productivity, to the corporate image, to community relations or to assist the sales effort. That is what this short paper set out to prove.

Why Communicate with Employees?

It started by asking this question. It then attempted to answer it by pointing out that, if an organisation – any organisation – serves a customer base, if it operates in a competitive environment, or if it has employees who meet customers or other opinion formers, then that organisation needs to communicate with its employees.

Those three factors were seen as being crucial to the continued well being of any organisation, public or private. If it does not communicate properly, the argument continued, employees – at most levels – will not be able to:

- represent the best aspects of the organisation to customers;

- present a competitive edge – partly, but not wholly, applicable in the private sector;

- create a good impression on customers and opinion formers.

The classic argument here is that an organisation of, say, 12,000 employees, automatically has 12,000 ambassadors. Some will be good, some bad, the majority somewhere in between, but mostly tending to the mediocre. All of them are only as good or as bad as their views of the organisation that employs them.

> All our workforce are ambassadors and, therefore, they need to know where they are and how they fit into the organisation. We are a thinking caring body and it's important that people recognise that.

> (Town Clerk, Corporation of London.)

The RMC report went on to quote from an industry-wide committee report:

> There is proof that effective employee communication benefits

company and individuals alike; it improves performance, helps the company to survive and increases the security and commitment of individuals to the company. Major specific benefits of effective employee communication include:

- an improved industrial relations climate;
- an increased awareness among employees of company activity and plans;
- a better method for employees to make – and management to hear – suggestions about the company's plans and policies and their implementation on the shop floor;
- the opportunity for the company to use fully the accumulated experience of all employees;
- an enhanced role for line managers;
- a more positive attitude to change within the company;
- the opportunity to solve problems before they become crises.

("Guidelines for In-company Communications" The Constructional Steelwork Economic Development Committee.)

What does Good Employee Communications Achieve?

This was the next question that the report asked and attempted to answer. From the evidence assembled for the report, it seems fairly clear that we can draw the following conclusions about good employee communications.

- It creates and sustains employee commitment.
- It concentrates effort on the task in hand – achieving the company's objectives – rather than on internal wrangling.
- It improves efficiency by clearly defining employees' roles and arms them with relevant information to enable them to carry out those roles.
- It empowers employees to represent the company in the best possible light.
- It enhances levels of customer service.
- It acts as an essential tool in coping successfully with change.

Committed employees, runs the argument, are very good PR value, let alone all the HR factors. They are also a priceless asset in the drive for better customer relations. In this and in other spheres, they can have a major effect on bottom line and this is borne out by First Direct Bank which estimates that 25 per cent of its new customers come through positive recommendation based on the way in which its employees handle existing customers.

Holderbank, a Swiss based, pan-European company involved in cement aggregates, concrete and concrete chemicals, was voted the *Financial Times'* most respected company in the construction sector in 1996. One of the reasons for this was its use of the argument that it is an environmentally responsible company; much of this message was put across by some of its 44,000 employees to their respective stakeholders in countries all over the world. It had sales of nearly US$7 billion in 1995, not a bad advert for strong employee communications.

It is also relevant to look at the increasing respect being given, in countries such as the UK, to Investors In People (IIP) which is a prime champion of the need to communicate effectively internally.

IIP National Standard

An extract from this standard, which is rapidly assuming ever-wide credibility throughout the developed world, is:

> 1. An 'Investor In People' makes a commitment from the top to develop all employees to achieve its business objectives.

Assessment Indicators

> 1.1 The commitment from top management to train and develop employees is communicated effectively throughout the organisation.
> 1.2 Employees at all levels are aware of the broad aims or vision of the organisation.
> 1.3 The organisation has considered what employees at all levels will contribute to the success of the organisation and has communicated this effectively to them.
> 1.4 Where representative structures exist, communication takes place between management and representatives on the vision of where the organisation is going and the contribution that employees and their representatives will make to its success.

> (This is one of four main assessment indicators considered for all IIP applications.)

At the time of writing, in 1998, the most recent available figures showed that 7,643 organisations had gained recognition as IIP in the UK, covering over 2 million employees. A further 28,775 organisations are committed to achieving the standards which will cover a further 6.6 million employees. Together, these figures represent 73 per cent of organisations employing over 200 people. At just 10.4 per cent of eligible organisations, the construction industry is the least committed of all the major industry sectors (figures as at 3 August 1997).

Furthermore, there is the very valid point that employees can do their job better if they know what is going on in the organisation.

> A successful organisation should . . . regularly communicate results and share information, enabling individuals to know what's expected of them and how they are doing.
>
> (Professor Jeffrey Pfeffer, Professor of Organisational Behaviour, Stanford University. "The Pfeffer Lecture", Barbican October 1995.)

But UK and US experts are not alone in this type of interpretation of the need for enhanced employee enfranchisement. There is an increasing realisation of its worth throughout other areas of the world. For example:

> Suddenly we were faced with competition and huge technological advances; we were good technically but not good in terms of service and efficiency. We were over staffed, we confused activity with results and we carried lots of fat. We needed to cut the crap, de-layer the organisations, improve the service and make life simpler for internal and external customers. It is an agonising process.
>
> (Linus Cheung, Chief Executive, Hong Kong Telecom, 1998.)

Maybe lots of organisations need to "cut the crap" and de-layer themselves. Yet this is one of the hardest management decisions, never mind the logistics involved in carrying out that decision. Partly because most of us hate to admit that we're beaten, partly through vested interest, the decision to de-layer is painful – an admission of failure and the removal of professional and, sometimes, financial security.

Because of this, it is often left to succeeding generations of senior management to take this decision and to follow it through with hard but practical action. And both these phases – decision and action – need to be very carefully communicated internally and externally, otherwise the slimming down process can reach lemming proportions and run away with the entire organisation.

This is not a particularly new revelation. As long ago as the great depression in 1932, the US conglomerate, Johnson & Johnson was writing that:

> If it becomes necessary to discipline employees, they should be told 'why' and be given every chance to be heard.

Yet, as recently as 24 October 1996, we read that over 200 employees of a US company called ADFlex Solutions Inc. had to read about their forthcoming redundancies on the Internet. According to the *London Evening Standard* on that day:

> Workers discovered that their factory was moving from Hampshire to Thailand with the loss of more than 200 jobs – after logging on to the Internet.

> ADFLex Solutions Inc. plans to save hundreds of thousands of pounds a year by centralising production in the Far East where staff are much cheaper.

> But the first some employees at the company, in Havant, knew of the closure was when they read a statement issued on the firm's Internet site.

Impressed? You wouldn't be if you had worked for ADFlex Solutions Inc.

What can Happen when an Organisation does not Communicate with Employees?

The RMC report went on to ask the above question, and the answer has to be: "Quite a lot, actually, much of it not very desirable."

For a start, employees become confused about what they should be doing and why. They tend to regard everything they can as somebody else's job and to wait for somebody else to do it.

Uninformed employees do not understand how their work contributes to the overall business of the organisation – or, indeed, whether it does contribute at all. If there is no feeling of contribution, no sense of value in what they do, no matter how small, pride in their work vanishes as quickly as snow off a dyke. Once pride has gone, it takes a very long time, a lot of hard work and, often a good deal of budget that could have been spent on something else, to bring it back again. In the meantime, all sorts of negative things could have happened, especially in a commercial situation.

Customer confidence, market share, quality of product or service, sales volumes, profit margins, management and investor confidence and self-belief can all disappear with frightening rapidity once the downward spiral has been triggered by uncaring and uninformed employees.

Employees are not empowered to represent the organisation in a good light – because they don't know the facts. When they don't know the true facts, they begin to make them up. When that happens, the jungle telegraph fills the void and rumour rules the employee's mind.

Disaffected employees make very negative ambassadors and very bad news headlines – as any half-decent PR practitioner will agree. There is a cliche that "today's clock notice is tomorrow's headline". It was used extensively during the early-1980s when the media spotlight was firmly on industrial relations issues, especially disputes, but it still applies today, Now, however, it should probably refer to "today's headline", so instantaneous is the broadcast media.

Here is an example, necessarily anonymous, of the lack of communications efficiency in a major public sector body in the mid-1990s:

> There are poor communications between departments; there's no commonality of purpose and rivalry can develop. My department wasn't considered important, so I've had to try to increase its credibility.
>
> Paper communication is very slow; it can take five days for a memo to come down three floors.
>
> (CEO, leading public sector body.)

Never mind that memos are outdated; it can take just as long for people not to switch on their e-mail if they feel like it. The point here is not the mechanical delivery of the message; it's the will to communicate that is important together with the belief that internal communications is critical to the health of the organisation.

Stress

On top of all this, poor communications with employees is now recognised as one of the four main causes of work-related stress. A CBI survey shows that inefficiencies arising from stress costs up to 10 per cent of the UK's gross national product – or £3.7 billion (Health and Safety Executive (HSE) figures, September 1996).

Therefore, individual organisations can assume that 10 per cent of their turnover inefficiency factor is similarly caused by stress, of which at least one quarter is due to poor employee communication.

Some aspects of the British Health and Safety Executive, a government body, relating to this point are now covered by legislation under both criminal and common law. This legislation is even more formidable when it is Europe-wide, as much of it is now becoming under the auspices of the EU. When it was purely national, there were often loop holes or blind eyes, now these are rapidly being closed – or opened – depending on your point of view.

The British Institute of Personnel and Development's (IPD) blueprint for occupational health and organisational effectiveness includes the need to "communicate the need for a mission initiative, what is to be achieved and how it will be done". These are directly related to the goals of "reducing costs, increasing output, winning contracts, complying with statutes and achieving safe working systems". (Institute of Personnel and Development Bulletin September, 1996.)

In this context, health issues can impact upon any employee, not just those on the receiving end of the communications process. The closure of the MG plant at Abingdon was a dramatic and highly visible case of internal communication that was badly handled until it was too late. One very senior director's health was so badly affected by the whole exercise that he had to be retired early on health grounds.

Mobility and sick leave are indicators of a happy staff.

(Senior Manager at the Corporation of London.)

Equally, of course, they can be very telling indicators of an unhappy staff. There is also the potential for reducing the threat of industrial unrest. Just look at this short example:

. . . if a local (industrial relations) dispute seems likely, the Association's HQ has to contact the establishment division who have to contact the controller of operations who has to contact the regional office who has to contact the prison governor. The governor is not allowed to talk directly with the people involved in a local dispute.

(Prison Officers' Association, Employee Communications in the 1980s, Michael Bland.)

Thus, attitude barriers develop based on misunderstanding, misinformation, rumour, media speculation, external body sources, etc. These attitude barriers can be lethal in that they perpetuate myths and false assumptions, reduce commitment and enthusiasm, create a climate of suspicion and sulkiness and reduce the constructive effort of the employee. Worse, it often leads to conflict in the workplace, which is expensive and uncomfortable for all involved.

What Kind of Communication do Employees Need?

Managers, especially, need information to enable them to carry out their jobs better – e.g. data on quality, sales, customer satisfaction, audit results, financial performance, competitors' actions – and we will look at examples of this and the way in which some organisations approach this task later in the book.

Employees, however, need more than practical information; they also need inspiration and leadership. They need information to make them believe in and trust the organisation as an entity in which they are willing to entrust their future security and that of their families. This means that they need open communications, honesty of approach, evidence of positive aspects such as community involvement, investment in the future, job security and sound financial results, if appropriate. Ignorant employees breed suspicion and dissatisfaction and these diseases are both highly contagious.

Too often, however, the fundamentals are seemingly ignored. In reality, the essence of internal communications is very simple. Does it appear so in your organisation? If so, it is a good and responsible organisation. The basics are set out with clarity and simplicity in the following extract:

> Emphasis on communications has three main aspects:
>
> * establishing direct channels between employer and workforce;
> * cascade and team briefing systems;
> * employees are given the big picture of business goals and circumstances.
>
> This has resulted in a sustained and visible commitment which holds up well in times of stress, e.g. financial difficulty, job losses or takeover.
>
> (Cave, *Managing Change in the Workplace* Coopers & Lybrand, 1994.)

Coopers & Lybrand is among the very best at internal communications – and it has the comparative disadvantage of having extremely highly educated and well-informed audiences to whom to communicate. It's much easier to tell people something they don't know than something that they think they know already.

It is also much easier to communicate with employees of a more limited ambition; they are content with less information because they understand less information. In certain circumstances, the more they are told, the more confused and concerned they can become. Some employee versions of annual results fall into this category. Although they mean well by trying to interpret the, often complex, sets of figures into understandable soundbytes for those who, like me, failed O level Maths, they can sometimes end up creating more uncertainty than existed before.

One of the great entrepreneurs of the 1980s puts a characteristically salty interpretation on it:

> It is my view that unions were only needed when management were bastards . . . Nothing has been more important to The Body Shop's success than our ability to communicate with our staff at all levels. I took the view that it did not matter a hoot how much I knew about The Body Shop if I was unable to communicate my views to other people . . . We communicate with passion – and passion persuades.[1]

---

1. Anita Roddick, *Body & Soul* (1991).

Another great British captain of industry is just as direct:

> Making it happen means involving the hearts and minds of those
> who have to execute and deliver . . . These are not the people at
> the top of the organisation but those at the bottom . . . nothing will
> happen unless everyone down the line understands what they are
> trying to achieve.[2]

Two more examples serve to heighten the point:

> Marks & Spencer is the most obvious example of the philosophy
> of good communications in action. Communicating first and fore-
> most with its own employees has given this company the confi-
> dence to describe its entire work force as members of its PR team.[3]

> The objective of communication is to help management to con-
> duct the affairs of the enterprise with the maximum effectiveness
> in the use of all resources . . . The aim of communication is . . . to
> see that the right people get the information that they should get.[4]

It's very difficult to argue with the logic of any of those extracts, yet how
many organisations can honestly say that they regularly and effectively carry
out activities which put these policies into practice? If yours can, then your
job is worth hanging on to.

Is this all Employees Need?

This was the next aspect of the RMC report. It concluded that, as has been
observed, some employees do not need detailed data; they need reassurance
about the company and their role in it. Particularly, they need to know:

• that the company has a future;

• that they have a future with that company;

• what they can do to safeguard that future;

• how they can contribute to future security.

Trusting employees will overlook the odd mistake and ignore or refute negative rumour, thereby helping the PR effort considerably.
　　Increasingly, there is the temptation to rely on new technology to do the

---

2. Sir John Harvey-Jones, *Making it Happen* (1988).
3. Theon Wilkinson, *The Communications Challenge* (1989).
4. Alec Irvine, *Improving Industrial Communication* (1970).

job. This is usually misguided; developments such as e-mail do not necessarily communicate for managers. For instance, a well-known computer company has 94,000 employees worldwide; they are all on e-mail. They send each other, on average, 2 million e-mail messages every month.

Yet, a recent survey showed that knowledge of the company and trust in the management was at an all time low point.

It is difficult to demolish the argument that too many managers hide behind new technology and use it as an excuse not to communicate. Professional communication is a two-way process in three classic stages:

- clarify the message;

- ensure it has been understood by the audience;

- ensure the audience has a right of reply.

If just one of these areas is not present, communication has not taken place. Communication is not about glaring at a screen; it is about eyeball to eyeball dialogue – even if that means glaring at the other eyeball.

> The Meat Training Council is concerned that many of its members are facing extinction. Before the obvious reasons connected with health arose, they identified five major causes, one of which was poor internal and corporate communications. The subsequent confusion over mad cow disease proves the point.[5]

The Importance of Communicative Leadership

This will be discussed in more detail later, however, any organisation without leadership is likely to slide into anarchy. Human behaviour nearly always wants to be guided in a positive way. This way can only be achieved through arriving at a constructive, creative, collaborative working environment in which consensus, not conflict, is the order of the day.

In this environment, individuals can meet their personal and professional goals, fulfil the roles expected of them in the company context and contribute more fully to its success.

For example, Rover Cars now claims to have got its employee communications so far advanced that it receives over 35,000 practical suggestions each year about how the company could do things better. That kind of treasure chest of knowledge was denied to the management in the past, largely because they had given up managing because they had stopped communicating.

---

5. *MEAT the Challenge* Meat Training Council (January 1996).

Two other examples extend this point:

> I would appreciate people thinking that their work might affect others.
>
> (Corporation of London.)
>
> There needs to be a focused, positive approach to employee com-munications . . . so that organisations succeed by raising skills, using these to differentiate products and services, and earning, by excellent customer service, high profits, high earnings and as se-cure a future as can be managed . . . this vision embraces em-ployee voice. Good employee communication practices . . . lead to commitment, job satisfaction and a willing contribution . . . higher productivity and profitability . . . partly by listening to the voice of the employees.
>
> ("Employment Relations in the 21 Century" IPD, December 1997.)

Employee communications is also effective because:

- it enhances employee commitment;
- good calibre staff at all levels tend to remain loyal longer;
- the longer staff remain, the lower the staff turnover;
- recruitment is expensive; the lower the turnover, the more money is saved.

In the late-1980s, for instance, a subsidiary of Saatchi & Saatchi in London had a staff turnover of around 45 per cent per annum. This cost a huge amount of money – such as executive time in interviewing, selecting, appointing, advertising, induction courses, training, etc. Most senior and middle manag-ers spent a great deal of their time trying to sort out either people or money. In the process, a few clients got left by the wayside; others decided to look elsewhere. The result was a radical shake-up, a reorganisation and, eventu-ally, a merger with another agency and the forcible removal of most of the original senior staff, some of whom were clearly perceived to have been in-capable of managing their employees professionally.

Now, employee turnover – helped by a tougher employment market in that particular sector – has fallen to around half the 1988 levels and, as a consequence, recruitment costs have fallen substantially.

Empowerment

Empowering employees is a buzz phrase at the moment – and is consequently, over used and often warped out of context. However, like many buzz phrases it has its genesis in common sense:

> What we need to look for now are the communicating circumstances that encourage employees to give their creativity for the benefits, not just for themselves, but for the organisations that employ them. The sensible employer includes the following policies:
>
> - providing as much information as possible and communicating effectively;
> - getting people involved in making decisions about their work and having the responsibility to do so to maximise efficiency and performance.
>
> A climate of trust between management and workers and a commitment to employee communications and involvement are critical.[6]

> A workforce which knows roughly what is going on within its organisation is more likely to have confidence in that organisation, themselves and their future. Consequently they're much less likely to do something daft. They realise what they've got to lose. They are also likely to be prepared to work harder and more conscientiously – which usually results in higher and more consistent levels of quality in what they are doing.[7]

Community Relations

This is one of the most important aspects of corporate life at the beginning of the new millennium. There is a strong feeling, especially in financial circles, that the days of the 1980s, when organisations were judged purely on the bottom line, have gone for good. Investors at both institutional and individual level now want to see a demonstration of responsibility to society as a whole and, particularly, to the individual communities in which they carry out their operations.

The leading UK newspaper, *The Times* (known in olden days as 'The Thunderer' for its outspoken attitude to government and the establishment) runs a corporate profile column every week in which it assesses organisations on a number of factors. These are:

---

6. Professor John Purcell, Department of HR Management, University of Bath (April 1997).
7. Greener, *Secrets of Successful PR* (Butterworth-Heinemann: 1991).

- ethical expression;
- fat-cat quotient;
- financial performance;
- share performance;
- attitude to employees;
- strength of brand (if any);
- innovation;
- annual report;
- city star rating;
- future prospects.

A PR person's nightmare if the findings on the ethical and related topics are not all that they should be. An independent consultant, somewhat idealistically named "Integrity Works", advises *The Times* on the ethical considerations and examines aspects such as standards of business conduct, approach to values from top to bottom and business principles expressed and continually monitored in line with best practice.

Another independent consultant, Crisp Consulting, advises *The Times* of fat-cattery – that is, analysing the organisation's attitude to senior managers' overt and covert remuneration. It looks out for aspects such as pay levels, pay rises, share options, comparative packages in other organisations, pay-offs and perk levels. In other words, park your Rolls around the corner if you think you are going to be investigated.

Clearly, all this type of scrutiny is not lost on employees – and neither are the published reports. Indeed, employees themselves have a role to play in helping to compile the evidence for the reports – especially in the section on 'attitude to employees' which *The Times* is far too wily to take purely on the word of the Head of HR or whoever they are listening to. If the expressed attitude is not borne out in fact, that organisation can end up with a very red face on the Monday morning when the report appears, especially as all the board members are listed by name.

Researching Attitudes

Consequently, more time – and a little more money – is being spent in finding out what employees think about their employers. In the process, organisations also discern what an employee is likely to tell a reporter. It would be encouraging to think that this increased effort would be spent anyway, without the added incentive of vehicles such as *The Times*' 'Corporate Profiles'.

Notable examples of UK companies carrying out – and acting on the findings of – regular attitude surveys include BA, Birmingham Midshires Building Society, Rank Xerox, UK Atomic Energy Authority. So do many more, far too numerous to list here.

But, the important point about the handful of companies quoted above is that all of them also canvas their customers and communities about the staff with whom they deal in order to help maintain a high level of customer and community relations. In other words, they don't leave it to chance. They check that what is supposed to happen in employee and community relations terms, does happen, at least most of the time in most of the cases monitored.

Committed staff can achieve wonders in community relations terms that can otherwise be very expensive. For instance, in the late-1980s, a chemical factory was emitting fumes which burnt holes in the washing hung out on washing lines in neighbouring back gardens. Although housewives objected, the small town depended on the factory for work. Most of the employees got together with management and community bodies to resolve the situation quickly, quietly and inexpensively. The story was successfully kept out of the media. Only a handful of people in the company and the community concerned will now even remember it – yet it could have been a classic crisis management case study.

The impact of strong internal communications on positive community relations will be examined in more detail later in the book.

Committed Staff also make it easier to Recruit Good Calibre Employees

This sounds self-evident; so do many aspects of internal communications once they are written down. Finding them spelt out in black and white, however, is often elusive.

For example, one large engineering company in the Midlands had a very disaffected workforce, which systematically put off potential graduate recruits from accepting a job with the organisation because they believed they owed it to their consciences. One of the previous year's graduate intake, for instance, was unwisely trotted out to greet potential graduate recruits in order to advise on what life was like working for the company.

When asked what kind of work he did, he snorted and replied: "Read magazines mostly. There's nothing else to do. To be frank, nobody here has the faintest idea of what to do with me or any of the other graduates. I wouldn't advise you to join this lot; they don't know what they're doing or why they employ people."

The company was almost bankrupt through lack of competent staff to run its factories. Eventually, it had to be financially restructured; banks and other financiers took over. Immediately, 9,000 direct jobs were lost with 15,000 more indirect jobs going as a result.

Organisations with highly committed staff – such as Mars – make it easier for those staff to pick the cream of the talent and to keep it harnessed to the company over the long-term – the golden handcuffs approach which is based on far more than money.

Positive induction courses of new staff that pay due attention to communications issues are equally important. For example:

> When I arrived, I didn't get to meet anyone senior. Induction was needed because I had to discover everything the hard way, to try to put faces to signatures. I had to ask questions about uncertainties, I needed a guide to overlaps of responsibility.

(Head of Department, Corporation of London.)

Good News/Bad News

Good communications make it easier to communicate bad news successfully – with a lower risk of negative action and publicity and an increased chance of getting positive stories covered because the organisation has a reputation for good communication both internally and externally. Apart from the odd hiccup, when did you last see sustained negative coverage for, say, Marks & Spencer? The company has spent much time, effort, ingenuity and resource in developing a strong corporate image, based partly on employee communications. This has delivered consequent support for the organisation, empowerment for employees to talk about it knowledgeably and positively to its publics and stakeholders and a further elevation of the image itself. A rare example of a highly successful policy in which everyone gains – the classic South East Asian win-win policy.

Competitive pressures, such as the need to balance the needs of investors, customers, employees and business partners, mean that news can be bad in any organisation, whether public or private sector, anywhere in the world.

Furthermore, if the bearer of negative news – the internal communications team – is trusted and respected, the reaction will usually be disappointment rather than anger; responsibility rather than irresponsibility.

Because of all this, many organisations are now specifically building internal and employee communications. The following extract is from a UK Housing Association board paper which is headed "Annual Review of Strategy" and is dated 4 February 1998.

5.5   Better Communication

> Most organisations now recognise the need for good communications. In [our Association] our geographical spread and the nature of the customer services pose particular problems. As part of improving our communications we intend that:

5.5.1 Our new IT system will be linked between all offices to enable work to be performed in different locations, to have e-mail and intranet facilities and to improve telephone and other links.

5.5.2 Our administrative systems and staffing skills will be over-hauled to improve contact and quality of employee com-munications.

5.5.3 Team briefing systems should be further improved in the year ahead.

5.5.4. We should continue with communication tools such as staff forums, staff conference day, middle manager/senior man-ager quarterly meetings, attendance at board meetings for key staff.

Put more succinctly, let us finish this brief look at the sound reasons for adopting strong internal communication by quoting from the Communica-tion Policy of Schering Health Care, one of the foremost international play-ers in its field. The following communication policy statement is for every-one who works for Schering Health Care.

It is company policy to ensure that you receive all the information you need to enable you to do your job.

The company will also ensure that you share a wider perspec-tive of departmental and company issues, recognising that job sat-isfaction, morale and performance can be positively influenced as a result.

The company will maintain communication channels which will enable you to understand and influence the environment in which you work. The company will encourage you to participate in two-way communication processes.

Blindingly simple, obvious once read, but still unusual in its insight and clar-ity. It could become an object lesson for many other organisations.

CHAPTER FOUR

The Modern Manager

Whose Job is it?

One of the most pressing questions concerning modern internal communications is, who, exactly, should be doing it? Is it the preserve of the HR function, still known as 'personnel' in some organisations and, graphically, as 'human remains' in others? Is it a responsibility of the PR function that is probably regarded as something of an interloper by the more traditional HR staff? Is it a halfway house, an internal communication function, with a foot in both camps? Is it the senior management of an organisation, on the basis that only they can tell when the time is right to communicate information that could be of a highly sensitive nature? Or is it the line manager who is responsible for facing his or her employees every working day and feels that they are entitled to know more about the organisation and, indeed, to have a better understanding in order to help them carry out their jobs more effectively?

As with most riddles, there is no easy answer, although there are many wrong ones. Moreover, any attempt to answer the question at all is bound to incur the disapproval of at least some, if not all, of these groups. All organisations are different; what is a right strategy in one may not work at all in another for very valid reasons. The interpretation of the positions involved in internal communications also differs widely from one organisation – and indeed, one sector – to another. There is, in short, no panacea to the thorny question of who it should be.

HR

To take the leading candidates in turn, the HR function has the benefit of occupation of the role in many organisations. This is not always an advantage to anyone other than the HR department, however. It may be impertinent but it could also be pertinent to ask why, since HR functions – or their personnel ancestors – were responsible for internal communications for so long, certainly in the UK, has the practice got into such a mess of neglect and ineptitude? There have been plenty of examples furnished already in the preceding chapters to demonstrate the dire state of internal communications in a number of organisations and, in the absence of any other convincing evidence, it is tempting to believe that these are relatively typical of many others.

I have nothing against HR people and much of what they do is very good work – but are they all natural communicators? Do they always have a strategic grasp of the organisation's needs in terms of staff motivation, employee commitment and all the rest of it? If they have, why are they still HR staff?

The trouble seems to be that word 'traditional'. For decades, being a personnel manager meant all sorts of things, many of them dreary but necessary, such as wage negotiations, industrial relations, selection and recruitment, induction and training, welfare, health and safety, keeping abreast of employment law and attempting to interpret it for the organisation, adjusting staffing levels to finance departments' demands, or else providing fitting evidence as to why they should not. All this is very 'worthy' work – someone has to do it – but 'worthy' can be used, and often is among management thinkers, as a pejorative. At best, it is not very exciting work and perhaps because of this, it has traditionally not attracted a very exciting sort of person.

There's nothing wrong with that either. It would be a terribly superficial world if everyone were to be exciting, far more exasperating than if everyone were catatonically dull, but, the question has to be asked whether or not internal communications people need excitement in their make-up. I think they do.

A lot of internal communications is all about selling concepts, policies and changes. Some of them are uncomfortable; others may not actually be uncomfortable but may be perceived to be so. In either case, it can be a difficult and very sensitive task. It can be a task that needs an element of sales, of marketing and of hype. If you look at recruitment adverts for internal communications staff, you will often see phrases such as:

> . . . you will be responsible for designing and implementing an effective internal communication strategy, using a wide variety of media which will include in-house newspapers, notice boards, videos and booklets.

Wow, notice boards. Gripping stuff. This is taken from an actual advert in December 1997 and it does not exactly request excitement. Consequently it is unlikely that any terribly exciting people applied. Even if they did, the chances are that they were a bit too exciting for the organisation which played safe and promoted old Jones (or Smith) from HR (or purchasing) because he only had a few years to go and it would save an early retirement package.

This is the problem with some HR people as internal communicators. If they do not exude excitement from every pore of their being, unless they actively go out of their way to break the mould and re-create the internal communications function in the spirit of dynamic, exciting, fresh and memorable communication, the expectations of them from both their peers and their audiences is likely to be rather low key. Often, this is the case.

Unless communications are made exciting, the audiences won't bother to look at them. We are all, each and every one of us in the UK, subjected to an average of 180 advertising messages every single day of our lives. That's a lot of competition. Advertising agencies employ highly creative – and often highly paid – people called 'creatives' to make us look at or listen to those messages. Against this background, the average traditional HR manager has very little chance of creating excitement, and yet that is what the role calls for.

The problem is that, if a message is not received and understood by its audience, it has failed. So, by implication, has the function that thought of it in the first place. A message, which doesn't get across to its audience, cannot be defined as having been successful and, if the right elements of creativity, packaging, imagination and excitement are not present in those messages, they will not get across.

PR

PR is a funny sort of animal in management terms. Barely old enough to vote but often throwing down the gauntlet with a clamorous brashness, it can seldom be ignored for long; it's the spotty adolescent profession in comparison with the well-established, even hoary headed old stagers, such as law and accountancy. Consequently it tends to be given less regard which it should, in theory, command.

Nevertheless it has its uses, one of which is the ability to communicate professionally, convincingly and persuasively with its organisations' audiences. Indeed, if the PR function cannot do this, there is little point in retaining it, for that is its purpose in life. Whether it be damage limitation in a crisis or embarrassing situation that has (or could) got into the public domain or whether it is to massage opinion along desired ways of thinking, PR has grown uncommonly quickly over the last 30 years and is now here to stay, at least in some guise.

Moreover, its very essence is creativity; not in the pretty picture sense but in the sense of taking a message, or series of messages and making of them something palatable, credible, rational and understandable – no mean feat considering some of the organisations for which PR people work. This may be carried out through a variety of methods but one common link often spans the spectrum – the ability to write clearly, concisely and very quickly. Some PR people, though not necessarily the best ones, are ex-journalists and the two professions have this in common, that they are paid on their ability to write. The difference is that the journalist will write what is in the best interests of the readership of his or her publication; the PR person will write what is in the best interest of his or her organisation.

This skill is in demand. Take another two extracts from adverts for internal communications managers:

Educated to degree standard with writing experience ideally gained in a journalistic capacity, you will have strong creative skills which will support the ability to think strategically.

Not the ideal profile for an HR person perhaps although it fits the bill for an internal communications manager better than the previous advert.

Selecting and reviewing the most appropriate communication channels, including Business TV, videos and . . . publications among others, will be essentials. You should be a communications professional with at least three years experience in internal communications, gained ideally within a dynamic changing business environment and be used to advising senior executives and delivering workable solutions under pressure.

There are some skills specified here that are not exactly associated with HR people. A knowledge of broadcast media – albeit internally – is one. A communications professional is another. Delivering solutions under pressure is a moot point; HR people work under pressure like anybody else. However, if they were to experience the kind of pressure cooker pressure under which journalists and some PR people operate regularly, they may well find it something of a culture shock. The term 'pressure' is relative and is not widely associated with HR functions in the minds of most managers I've met.

A third example underlines the point:

You should be a great communicator, both orally and on paper, with exceptional writing skills and serious attention to detail. You'll be expected to be both creative and commercially astute in your approach to issues and sensitive to the needs of individual businesses.

Again the emphasis is on professional communication – not a perceived core skill of the traditional HR function, except by default.

This type of advertisement, which is increasingly common, underlines perhaps the greatest change of thinking in the approach to internal communications of the 1990s. No longer is it enough to recognise the need. No longer is it enough to tackle that need with the conventional tools that would have sufficed (or not) in the 1970s and 1980s. Now it is widely regarded as imperative that the need is approached by a dedicated skill – that is communications – no matter what other issues prevail.

These communicators, sometimes but not always PR people, do not have to be experts in employment law or health and safety or industrial relations or even industrial psychology. All they have to do is to take the core message and communicate it by whatever means is appropriate so that the audience, the employees, understand and accept it. That sounds simple. Sometimes, it is; more often it isn't.

It also means that an internal communications person is sometimes only seen as being responsible for part of the process – the communicating bit. Others may devise the strategy for the communicators to communicate. Again, this position is changing. Now the input of the communicator is more widely accepted as being of use at, rather than after, the strategy formulation stage. There is a strong parallel with PR here too, in that PR people are now generally regarded as having a valid input to all aspects of communications strategies which would have been pretty rare twenty years ago. Perhaps the child really is father of the man.

Senior Managers

So we have professional HR and professional communicators – perhaps some form of PR people. The next category was the senior managers of an organisation, be they board directors, heads of department or corporate managers.

There is a double impact here. The first is that, without the full co-operation of these managers, the chances of a successful internal communications programme going ahead are extremely slim, virtually negligible. The second is that very few of these senior managers have the time to carry out the communicating themselves.

To take the first point first, senior management is pretty pressurised stuff. All that melodrama about it being lonely at the top is, or can be, absolutely true. Really senior managers hardly ever have a day to themselves, must exist on less sleep than a six month old baby and must have extremely understanding wives or husbands. In the middle of a crowded international schedule beset by jet lag, meetings, flights, meetings, dinners, meetings, board reviews, meetings, strategic forums and meetings, they hardly have any time to communicate internally. Do they? Yet, what is all this activity about but communication? Some of it will be external, admittedly, but the principle is still the same, as are the messages.

The external message should not, often, differ too much from the internal. There will be shades of meaning, degrees of detail perhaps, but the essence must be the same if credibility is to be maintained. So the senior managers are, in many cases, carrying out some of the basics of internal communications as a natural part of their jobs. A review meeting will usually involve staff other than those simply at board or heads of department level. That, in itself, is internal communications – to a point.

Moreover, senior managers may not be best served by being remote from their staff. It is terribly easy to become ideologically remote if contact is minimal or occasional and if staff lose sight of the direction of the organisation, in the public or private sector, because they no longer see the senior managers doing what they are paid to do – which is to manage. And a large part of that management is communications of one sort and another, much of it internal.

Yet, in how many organisations are managers assessed on their ability to communicate? How many organisations train their senior managers to communicate? How many of the managers themselves follow the example of Anita Roddick (which was given in Chapter 3) and set out to make communications a virtue in their organisations? All these are relevant questions and deserve a closer look in most organisations.

Line Managers

The task for line managers is even less easy – for them. Line managers are those in charge of a team responsible for carrying out a function, often away from the corporate centre of affairs, and they get the worst of both worlds. Very seldom are they told the full facts of a situation and yet they are expected to create and retain loyalty and enhance productivity through commitment.

This situation – line managers being expected to communicate but being given no help to do so – happens countless times a day. They cannot do the job by themselves, yet they are vital to the success of the entire communications package. Upon them rests the responsibility for performance in that unit; if they foul up, the chances are that there will be little opportunity to put it right and the pressure builds up accordingly.

Line managers, therefore, need more help than almost anyone else. They need this help in several forms. First, they need to be told why internal communications is important, what it contributes and how it is a part of their managerial responsibility – something along the lines of the arguments set out in Chapter 3. Second, they need to be trained in how to do it. It's all very well expecting a line manager to be a brilliant communicator, but very few are, especially if they are specialists in a totally different function, such as engineering, finance, computers or logistics. As an absolute minimum, they need to be trained in assertiveness, in presentation skills, in giving and receiving criticism and in handling meetings. They need to be trained in all kinds of other areas, too, writing skills, time management, stress management, interview techniques, a certain level of industrial psychology to help them to understand what their employees are going through and how best to help them through it.

They also need the ammunition to fire off. The clear, succinct messages from the corporate base, which tell the employees in clear detail what is happening, why and how and how they themselves can be part of it and contribute to its success. Line managers need to be given this information in writing, which they can then disseminate. Sometimes it is more practical in another medium, such as video, pulsed tape slides, e-mail, intranet, or in another form which will make it easier not only for them to understand it and pass it on, but also for the employees to understand and relate to their own situations.

Line managers are the sharp focus of cascades; they need to be empowered through information which is timely, accurate and expressed in a form which is easily understandable. Otherwise they are gravely hampered when it comes to carrying out the communications aspects of their managerial responsibility which forms a large part of their work.

What they don't need is to be left alone, expected to communicate as if by osmosis and then kicked for not having done so. A very large proportion of industrial disputes start because line managers are not empowered to communicate properly and therefore lose sight of the key managerial responsibility of keeping employees informed and harnessing their commitment for the good of the organisation.

Leading from the Top

There is also the political will to communicate as part of managing the organisation – whether in the private or public sector. Communication comes from the top; when it doesn't, it will fail. More often than not, when it does, it succeeds. But how do those charged with internal communications, whoever they may be, convince those at the top of the tree that it's time to start talking to one another a bit more?

Some of the answers lie in Chapter 3. They are the most common reasons for communicating and they have been proved in practice to have worked well in an organisation that was, at best, lukewarm and, at worst, openly hostile to the concept of communicating with its own employees in a much fuller and more honest manner.

The main arguments are set out there and it is unnecessary to repeat them here. But there are a few other arguments that can be applied on a more individual basis. For example, the main winners in a successful internal communications exercise are the people who are in overall control of the organisation just as much as the employees. If productivity, efficiency, cost effectiveness, quality, corporate image and financial viability are improved by the improved attitude and contribution of the employees, then top management are the first to know and benefit from this improvement.

Similarly, the employees themselves feel more useful or valued and more wanted in the psychological sense of the term. Most of us want to be wanted and valued by our organisations. We spend 75 per cent of our waking life at, or travelling to and from, work, That is too large a proportion to be wasted by negative attitudes that are forced by poor communications. By being brought into the culture, the ethos, the spirit (I hesitate to use the overworked and misunderstood word 'vision', but it's probably appropriate here) of the organisations, they feel as though they are part of it.

Here we come to the crux of the issue. If the employees cannot feel part of the organisation, they are not likely to want to stay. Look at the staff turnover rates quoted in Chapter 3; 45 per cent is a farce. Nobody can get on with any proper work because they're spending all their time, effort, energy and budget recruiting, organising induction courses and trying to retain staff. Heaven knows when – or if – the real work gets done.

Line managers have a major front-line role in this – the equivalent to the infantry officers, perhaps, or one of Nelson's ships' captains. They need the signals from the flagship and they need to know enough about the background strategy to be able to interpret those signals for their crew and to ensure that these are understood. Not just understood but that the reasons for them are clear, that the strategic logic is brought into clear focus and explained in simple terms; that it is something which all their crew can recognise, equate to and use to their benefit – so that it benefits the entire ship. A sense of belonging was never needed more than it is in this technocratic world which is running the danger of becoming too impersonalised.

In Nelson's day communities were tighter and more self-centred. Villagers usually knew each other intimately. There was very little commuting. Communities were much more self-contained and, as a consequence, people knew more closely where they fitted in and to whom they could turn for help. Organised religion was much stronger, the temptations of the outside world much less attainable. No television meant much smaller horizons and much less discontent.

The art of good managerial internal communications is to replace that community spirit with a new awareness of the entity that is the work unit. This is a role that can sometimes only be carried out by line managers; others can be too remote, too concerned with the bigger picture to be able to recognise the situation and use it to advantage. In this the line manager needs the support of the internal communications machine. That means senior management, HR, PR and any dedicated internal communications function there may be. So the task becomes a team effort and the line manager is supported by a strategy, a supply line and a logistics system that can enable him to do his or her role.

Internal Communications Functions

All of which brings us to the last category, the specialist internal communications unit. Where there is one, it is naturally the best solution. A fusion of the best of HR, PR and a number of other disciplines, it can change the face of internal communications in a short time, can harness much higher degrees of co-operation and can help to deliver commitment that could otherwise only be dreamt of.

Some of the skills needed have been quoted in the adverts above. It is only right that some of the desired qualifications should be quoted as well. For instance, we have phrases such as:

Educated to degree standard.

This is an obvious point and, increasingly, the real high fliers will also have a higher degree, often an MBA or equivalent and be proficient in a number of other aspects of communications, such as a marketing qualification, a modern language or a communications degree.

The ability to think strategically.

This, naturally, includes thinking strategically about the organisation and its context but also means thinking strategically about the whole global practice of internal communications and how it can be developed and channelled into improving the performance of the organisation.

Knowledge of the latest technology is a distinct advantage:
You will test and evaluate developments within the communications programme and adjust them accordingly.

This does not have to be purely a technological role, of course, but it almost certainly will include a strong element of technology and is not designed for latter day Luddites.

Rewards

Is this role which carries so many demands, rewarded appropriately? That depends on what you mean by 'appropriately'. The handful of job adverts quoted in this chapter, all date from mid-1998 and all offer salaries of £25,000-£30,000 plus the odd fringe benefit, although no cars, private health, non-contributory pension scheme, bonus or share options are specifically mentioned. And these adverts are for large, well-known organisations in thriving fields – finance, computers, engineering and so on.

Subjectively, this does not seem to be an outstanding reward for what could turn out to be a great deal of head bashing against the wall of senior management intransigence, employee apathy and a welter of confusion and mixed messages, especially in times of change management. Certainly, there are more badly paid jobs but equally there are many that require rather less intellectual application and professional effort and yet reward rather more generously.

Appropriate Professionalism

Internal communications professionals need to be the right type of managers as well. Too often in the past they have been leftovers from other functions whose days are numbered but who are deemed worthy of a last post in a role where they, apparently, can do little damage and less work. This is fatuous; they can do an irrevocable amount of damage in internal communications if they are not competent to carry out the role.

There is, for example, a public body that has very little idea of the need for internal communications – despite (or because of?) the fact that its chief executive is an ex-HR manager – and that has relied on a mixture of bullying, luck and blind faith on the part of its 20,000 employees over a long period of time. Two years ago, the task was entrusted to a secretary whose boss had taken early retirement and who herself had only eighteen months before retirement. Not surprisingly, she was hardly cut out for the task and despite her honest efforts to make a decent stab at it, the role was allowed to vegetate.

Now that she has retired – with heartfelt thanks that she never again has to try to come to terms with that foreign concept 'team briefing' – the body in question has decided, after having done nothing at all about internal communications for the interregnum, to cast around for another likely square peg. With brilliant foresight, they have hit upon a supernumerary who has led an itinerant life, rolling with equal disaster from one unsuitable role to the next, dabbling in at least four disparate departments in quick succession without ever seeming to understand what any of them were doing. Having nothing else for her to do, and needing to avoid another expensive early retirement for the sake of the political image, the body has decided to put her in charge of internal communications.

Set aside her lack of any appropriate qualifications, such as a degree, the ability to write concise, grammatically correct English, or even the skill of listening before talking, she is probably one of the most disliked and mistrusted officers in the entire organisation. Her background is hopelessly inappropriate and her educational and professional standing not nearly strong enough to tackle such a job. Her grasp of policy is virtually non-existent and her knowledge of the needs of the employees in terms of knowledge and information could be printed on the back of a postage stamp in double spacing. So she is the internal communications manager. Logical?

People can, of course, learn, but there must be a spark of some sort there in the first place. Just as creative writing can be developed but not inculcated where it never existed, there has to be some talent present in the make up of the internal communications officer if there is to be any real hope of success. As with any role, there has to be a fit between the person and their talent to the task needed. To identify a selling plate racehorse with a reputation for shying and an aversion to fences and enter it into the Grand National is not a sensible choice. Yet it is what too many organisations are doing.

Promotion from within is a laudable policy – when the skills are there or can be developed. Where they are not, there is little point in pretending that they are. That is simply ostrich management and there is far too much of that around as it is.

Although that example is in the public sector, it could have been in the

private sector, although it is probable that stark commercialism would pre-
clude it in most cases. The public sector seems to be especially unfortunate
in its inability to grasp the real needs of internal communications and to put
relevant, qualified talent in place to tackle the task. This is, of course, a generalisation and it may be very unfair on those public sector internal communications people who do a good job. But there is evidence time after time that
this is a generalisation with its feet firmly rooted in truth. Just ask your local
authority, health trust or government department what their internal communications policies are and what kind of staff carry them out, then wait for the
answer. Sometimes it will, no doubt, be valid; more often I suspect it will not.

Skill or Gift?

So, is internal communications a skill that can be learnt or is it a God-given
gift that cannot be replicated? Again the answer is not straightforward. Most
of the job is routine, common sense and organisational, all of which can be
taught, although some ground will no doubt be more fertile than the rest. But,
as the theme of the book so far shows, a great deal of the task is communications based and that means that managers have to be conversant with communications skills. Not only conversant but able to put them into practice,
which is a different thing entirely. You can admire an actor playing a part on
stage; to play that part yourself is a different matter. Yet that is what some
internal communications is all about.

But there are books and courses on communications skills in management; don't they enable managers to communicate better? Yes, some of them
do, and some are very good, but most are aimed at communicating one to one
in certain situations – redundancy, interviewing, assessing, appraising, etc.
They are not about communicating en masse to a group of employees at the
same time; they do not necessarily teach the gospel of good public speaking,
for example. Sometimes, these skills are common between individual and
group dealings; sometimes, they are not.

However, there are things we can learn from such sources and these indi-
cate the route along which all internal communications staff, especially line
managers, need to be trained. For example, one of the first requirements in
internal communications is often to gain accurate information about just how
employees feel about a certain issue. Setting aside the communications audit,
which we shall examine later, there is a skill in teasing this information out of
those employees who possess it but may not wish to divulge it.

Questioning Skills

To take an example at random, there are, for instance, several types of question beloved of HR managers: open, specific and closed. Open questions
allow the respondent to be as creative as he or she wishes. For example, a

questions such as: "What do you think of the new policy, product or manager?" gives great scope for developing a detailed answer; sometimes it can give too much scope and you begin to wish you'd never asked. It can often be elaborated in a digression or totally changed and taken off along a tangent which, although interesting, might not be what you want or need. On the other hand it allows the employee free rein to discuss all those aspects of the issues about which he or she feels most strongly and that in itself is a cathartic benefit which makes the employee feel that his/her opinion is being sought and listened to. It is useful to note down this opinion during the actual discussion so that there is the perceived likelihood that something will be done to act on the information; it may not actually be done, but at least the employee believes that it will be considered.

To be effective, this approach must consider the data it gains. There is nothing more depressing for an employee than to have an opinion canvassed and then to see absolutely nothing happen for years. This is an issue that constantly arises in communication audits. When talking to outsiders, such as external researchers or consultants, employees often let themselves go and freely relay all sorts of things that they are unlikely to tell their boss. Often they do this in the hope that somebody is listening and will try to make things happen as a result. If nothing ever does happen, which is all too often the case, not only is commitment and morale hit hard but that employee is spoiled for the next piece of research, thus queering the pitch for a considerable time.

The second type of question is the specific one, aimed at determining performance, responsibility, authority, even blame if there is a blame culture. For instance: "Whose responsibility is it to communicate with employees in A block?" This obtains vital knowledge in a convenient way (the answer must be either a name, job title or a profession of ignorance, all of which get us a little further into the maze) while at the same time, discovering the knowledge base of that employee. If he or she doesn't know, see how many others don't know either. If most of them don't, then what originally looked like a minor problem could actually be an epidemic.

The third type is the closed question, in which you can assess feelings, knowledge and assumptions. For instance, a question such as: "Did the production department meet the deadline?" can only result in one of two answers, either of which will shed light on the production department. In communications terms: "Have you seen this latest announcement about staffing levels in the R&D function?" also gives a very clear indication of what kind of information is getting through to what level of staff. The answer could have a profound effect on the need of the internal communication system. It can also be taken further by comparing relative knowledge in different departments and locations, thereby revealing more closely which managers are communicating and which are not. You probably suspected the truth, anyway, but this gives some empirical evidence on which to base a concrete policy.

Cross-checking can distinguish fact from opinion – often very useful in dealing with employees. Repeating some of the respondent's own phrases also shows that you are listening actively and are understanding what he or she is saying to the point of being able to repeat it accurately. Only do this if you can repeat it accurately, however; you will look fairly silly if you get it wrong and the respondent will think you are not listening or understanding, in which case considerable harm can be done.

That is another value of having an external researcher who can ask for amplification without looking stupid and who can ask what may appear to be very straightforward questions with no hidden agenda, although they may in fact be just as loaded, or even more so than those which would have been asked by in-house manager.

Now, there is nothing very hard or advanced in the skills just mentioned; they are pretty elementary and meat and drink to most people managers of any walk of life – or, at least, they should be. But how many line managers are actually trained in this type of issue? And how many are told how to make use of that information in designing and carrying out internal communications campaigns? Probably many more than was the case, say twenty years ago. Whether that is enough throughout a broad range of organisations is another matter.

Obtaining information is one thing. Presenting it is another question entirely. But it is a very valuable asset in the task of getting the best out of employees. In his annual Chartered Institute of Marketing lecture in May 1998, Tony Illsley, President of Walkers Snack Foods in the UK, said:

> To ignore the latent prowess of everyone in the organisation is downright bad business. We share information through round table initiatives and by developing managers as effective communicators so that they can work with their employees to find better ways of doing things. This is a two-way communications process and the first thing we had to do was to retrain most of our managers, especially line managers, in the art of team listening.

It must have worked. In three years at Walkers, Tony Illsley has presided over an increase in sales from five million to eight million packets of crisps a day. That's one in seven of the population buying a packet of his crisps every day. Not bad going.

Listening

Team listening is one way of ensuring that employees believe that their opinions matter, as we've just seen. Put simply, it means listening to employees' knowledge and distilling that input to extract the salient points which are worthy of further discussion and, maybe, of implementation in some form.

It's like a listening post crossed with a suggestion scheme and it has played a major role in the success of Walkers in finding better ways of doing things. Indeed, their internal marketing brand in this instance is "to find a better way" and it is this results-led effort in internal marketing and communication which has focused the group's efforts to increase sales and profits by around 60 per cent.

Listening is, of course, an essential aspect of communication – perhaps the most important aspect in many ways. People need to believe that you are listening to them before they will listen to you, although they won't often tell you that, especially if you are, ultimately, in control of their wage packets.

Putting the message across is another aspect of communicating that, quite needlessly, deters many line managers. We will look at the specifics and practical details in a later chapter, but the principle here is the same as the principle in eliciting the information in the first place. You need to explain the purpose of the process – what you're about and why. You need to present information in an ordered and logical way. This means marshalling your thoughts beforehand, sorting out the order in which you wish to raise issues, ensuring there is a logical progression in that order and then look at it from the point of view of the listener. How will they react? Will they understand what you are saying? If there is any doubt at all, then the sense needs to be made even clearer. Again, we will deal with the practicalities of this later.

Introducing new ideas out of the blue can be a major worry to employees, especially if those ideas could upset their relatively secure, relatively cosy world of work. Think back to your days as a junior manager. It takes long enough to work out a new job, to sort out in your mind and in the minds of other managers, how you fit into the scheme of things, what you can and can't do, how you can make a contribution that is within the remit of the job without rocking the boat. In many organisations and jobs, this comfort factor never happens. When it does it sometimes has to be bought in blood.

This factor is also the level at which many managers are happy to quit the ever upward spiral. It often tells them that they have reached their natural level on a kind of Archimedes management principle and that to try to get further up the tree would result in more hassle, more stress and pressure from others and from yourself and less leisure time with the family. It may not be worth it; if the motive is purely financial, it probably won't be.

Then, if someone comes along out of the blue – especially one of those dreaded consultants who know nothing about your organisation or its culture – and tells you that whatever you were doing was fine for last year but has to change again this year and implies that the cosiness you have laboured long and hard to build up is no longer a basis for your job security, you tend to get worried. Remember those days?

There was a graphic example in a police force in the late-1990s when external consultants were asked to advise on the type and structure of training that was being carried out internally. Since the annual training budget was £3 million, this was clearly a sensible decision, designed to channel public money correctly and to help enable the police to carry out their task of trying to make that particular county a safer and more pleasant place in which to live and work – their avowed mission.

The consultancy suggested that a survey be carried out of the training needs as they were perceived by the various officers at different levels who were the internal customers of the training department. Nothing unusual here, a kind of training needs analysis which is the first port of call of any self-respecting training consultancy and very much in line with conventional thinking. However, the suggestion provoked an outburst of pique, sulks, protest and lack of co-operation in the training department, mainly from one of the three full-time members of that department.

No matter how gently, tactfully or constructively the idea was presented to her by both the consultancy and her colleagues, her permanent stance was resistance at all costs. The result was that the idea was dropped and the police force in question may still not know whether the training it is providing is any use to those who receive it. Not a sensible use of hard won public money at a time of substantial lawlessness. (As an aside, the force in question spends more money rooting out police corruption than in fighting murder and robbery put together).

The fault, of course, lay largely with the management in not insisting politely but firmly that this review was carried out. Being polite and tactful is all very well, but sometimes employees need to be given an order, especially when there is the possibility of a hidden agenda in the offing. Good internal communications do not exist to perpetuate convenience, cosiness and complacency; those three 'c' words have no place in the future of a really vigorous organisation.

Again, the lead comes from the top; if those in authority set out a policy, then that policy needs to be communicated, discussed and implemented, not just communicated and discussed. Otherwise, management has ceased to manage.

New Ideas

Introducing one idea at a time is another way of gaining co-operation and can be very useful for the line manager. A deluge of new ideas can faze even the most resilient and innovative manager. Many lesser lights find even one hard enough to cope with but may get around to accepting it given time. Given two or more ideas and less time, there is little hope of anything but confusion and anxiety in their minds for a few weeks. Confusion and anxiety all too easily lead to resentment because employees don't understand the issues and feel ashamed of themselves for not doing so. This leads to aggression and resistance to whatever is being proposed – yet the original proposer may be blissfully ignorant that his or her idea has caused so much mental anguish in so many employees and their families.

Separating hard fact from management opinion is a finer shade of meaning and a nicer interpretation of logic but it is also necessary. It is one thing for a line manager to tell a workforce to do something because the management thinks it might be a good idea to try it. It is a much stronger message to prove the merit of that decision based on some of the stronger and more readily accessible information that supports the case.

A recent example of this is a health trust that wanted all its speech therapists to undertake training in complementary areas to try to maximise the value they were deriving from these employees. Speech therapists, being thin on the ground in the UK, can more or less walk into a job anywhere they like. The speech therapists in question resisted, because they didn't know why they were being asked to do this, because they felt affronted by the suggestion that they might not be professionally perfect and because they didn't feel like changing the relatively cosy way in which they were working – most were women whose part-time working patterns, while not earning a king's ransom, were convenient for family life.

After several months of wrestling to and fro with the ever more slippery problem, the health trust dropped the idea. Heaven knows what the U-turn cost in wasted management time and effort and a few external fees, but the outcome was precisely zilch. This happened at a time when waiting lists for medical treatment and hospital beds were growing to record proportions. What management got wrong was not the principle, which was perfectly valid, but the communications – in tactical, practical and emotional terms.

Emotions are lethal in communications. Yet they also form communications and that paradox is at the heart of many communication issues. Part of good internal communications is managing the feelings of those to whom you are communicating – all or some of your employees. Managing them, not to manipulate them, that is a different thing, but to achieve the desired outcome of the communications programme.

Recognition

This involves recognising the roles that you and they play within the organisation and how they are likely to react to the main thrust of the message. Trying to predict what they might say and do is key to successful communications and line managers especially need to know this. They also need to be trained in recognising that they too might have attitudes. Take it further; they may have prejudices, values and vested interests, which might affect the gist of the message, or the way in which it is likely to be received by its audience. This is all part and parcel of training line managers to communicate.

So is recognising how a message is being received – positively, negatively or neutrally. Too often, audiences give nothing much away and the communicator has to search for a reaction. In training it is a nightmare; the last thing the trainer wants is a room full of delegates sitting there like sacks of potatoes with never a flicker of emotion one way or another. The manager needs to identify clues that tell more about their reaction and what they are thinking as people (body language can often be invaluable here, but the manager, at any level, must be trained to recognise the tell-tale signs). Above all, he or she must be able to recognise the emotional appeals before the emotion becomes a problem – not afterwards. Then the police force situation can be avoided and there is a much greater chance of harmony being restored to a disturbed office without too many feathers being ruffled.

So, at the end of this chapter, have we decided who should be responsible for internal communication? HR, PR, senior management, line management, specialist internal communications units? Let Tony Illsley of Walkers have the last word:

> We don't have a communications manager; we don't even have a communications department because we all do it. Internal communications is a communal responsibility.

Just like the 1970s Japanese approach to quality and the much vaunted TQM concept, which panicked everyone in the West into all sorts of undignified and often fruitless cul de sacs, internal communications is everyone's responsibility – but, paradoxically, not everyone can do it, either in terms of skill or knowledge. That is where a co-ordinating unit comes in – and that is where the value of a dedicated internal communications function makes a great deal of sense as an investment in the future of the organisation.

CHAPTER FIVE

The Conceptual Approach

Before moving on to the practicalities of internal communications, it is necessary to look in more depth at the conceptual approach – what we are trying to achieve, what to communicate in general terms and to whom.

This chapter will look at these issues and also pay passing attention to aspects such as directional communications and the internal market in concept terms. The practical detail involved will then be examined in the following chapters.

What are we Trying to Achieve?

As we have seen in previous chapters, there are a number of benefits of good internal communications, seven of which are worth re-emphasising at this stage.

1. Dissemination of relevant, but not irrelevant, information.

2. Development of a communications culture leading to a culture of success.

3. Empowerment of employees to think creatively about their organisation.

4. Encouraging employees to contribute to the organisation in whatever way they can.

5. Equipping employees to act as positive ambassadors for the organisation.

6. Enriching employees' working lifestyles.

7. Encompassing employees in the organisational family.

These are all practical and beneficial outcomes of good internal communications, some of which we have encountered already. They bear a brief examination here to illustrate why the conceptual approach is so vital to the success of the overall internal communications effort.

Disseminating Information

The dissemination of relevant information is essential to allow most employees to do their jobs properly. It is the most fundamental of all managerial requirements – that employees are told what is expected of them, how, by when and perhaps, why. Even if the 'why' element is omitted, the remainder of the need holds good. Even a janitor cannot do his or her job properly unless he/she knows which loos to clean, when, where to get replacement towels and how to replace the disinfectant. This is relevant job information at its most basic. At the other extreme, a high-powered marketing team needs to know the corporate image properties of the organisation with which they work while briefing an external supplier to create a new campaign. The corporate image may not be explicit in the campaign but it must be there implicitly.

What neither end of this spectrum needs is irrelevance. A nursing sister at a recent management seminar grew very frustrated with a session about research and auditing. "I don't need to know this," she exploded. "It's all twaddle and it doesn't help my job. I stop people from committing suicide, I look after people in mental distress, which is part of everyday life. I don't need to know about research." She was wrong; a better knowledge of what drives people to suicide attempts might make her job a lot easier but she was too upset to view the issue logically. The trainer handled it very sensitively and the nurse left reasonably mollified but still totally convinced that research meant nothing to her.

Had the topic been presented to her as research into the causes of suicides, it might have attracted her attention more successfully. However, it would have been irrelevant to the other fifteen delegates who realised that knowledge is never wasted and that research into that knowledge might one day prove of benefit to their own roles.

Relevant information goes further than mere working tools. It can also encompass aspects of the organisation, which impact upon an individual – its properties, strengths, opportunities and policies. By communicating this information, a picture is built up in the employee's mind about what his/her organisation stands for – a sort of extended mission statement but far less crass. Only then can he/she really get down to the detail of committing to it or deciding to look elsewhere.

Committing means accepting its characteristics, warts and all. Not accepting those characteristics means that certain employees will never be truly committed to the role; they may occupy it while it suits them, they may be reasonably good at it, but they will never put their hearts and souls into it and that is the difference between an average employee and an outstanding one. It is the outstanding ones who make the difference when it comes to issues such as the competitive edge or the development of excellence. Average employees are only interested in themselves and their pay packets – jobsworths – and there are already too many of those in most societies and in most organisations without sloppy internal communications making matters worse.

Culture

If an organisation gets into the habit of communicating relevant information regularly and helpfully, it starts to create a communications culture. Employees will become accustomed to openness and sharing data; they will volunteer facts, pass opinions and even criticise others for not doing so. While this can lead to the odd difficulty, the benefits far outweigh the risks, since it is exactly this type of creativity which tends to break moulds and innovate – if not in product then in service, process, positioning, pricing and thinking. It is no coincidence that all these are areas can lead to exceptionally strong marketing strategies – the Walkers snack foods statistics quoted in Chapter 4 bear out this point.

A communications culture too is not so easily created that it can be taken for granted. One newsletter or team briefing will not automatically kick-start the process, but it is a start which can lead to better and greater achievements. Cultures are built gradually over a period of time, not overnight like an exhibition stand. Unfortunately, they can be destroyed overnight – Gerald Ratner is probably the outstanding example of recent years – and this destruction can be lethal to all involved. Yet, even this lemming-like process can be slowed down if a strong communications culture is in place. If other senior executives had known what Ratner was going to say at that fateful lunch, perhaps action could have been taken to stop him or to put in practice some other preventive measures.

Development of employee power is a direct result of the encouragement that strong internal communications can begin to help employees think creatively. The barriers to creativity tend to be fear of ridicule by colleagues and managers, uncertainty about whether the idea has been tried before, uncertainty about exactly what effect it would have in certain areas of the operation, a feeling that, if it is such a great idea, it must have occurred to others but, because it hasn't been put into operation, it clearly hasn't worked.

Good communications can remove most of these fears. Better information will allow employees to assess more accurately the effect their ideas have on colleagues and managers, other functions and the end product of the organisation. More relevant information can allow more informed and enlightened judgements to be made about a whole raft of effects connected with the issues about which employees are being creative. Indeed, they can spark off in the minds of employees enough new thoughts to break the inertia around the problem and start a new track of fresh thinking. It might not provide a panacea but it might suggest a few solutions.

It is partly through this enhanced creativity that employees can contribute more to their organisations. Remember President Kennedy's "think not what your country can do for you but rather what you can do for your country"? There is a strong parallel in internal attitudes; just substitute the word 'organisation' for 'country'.

Detail

It is also through closer attention to detail in employees' roles, checking the way in which their roles fit with others and ensuring that they give a better quality service that internal communications can make a telling contribution to any organisation. Yet this can also result in a more enthusiastic approach to their jobs – and enthusiasm is worth a great deal in most organisations. Certainly, it is worth a good deal in gaining and retaining a competitive edge and organisations with badly motivated employees tend not to be those at the leading-edge of anything except the guillotine.

For example, a small drinks company is currently struggling to survive and has several times gone through the hoop of appointing new senior managers. Without exception all these managers have decided to streamline the organisation by reducing staffing levels. No doubt this has reduced overheads but it has also greatly reduced the commitment and morale of the surviving staff. Employees are now so used to rumours of bad news – as well as the bad news itself – that they no longer try to come up with constructive ideas about how the company can get itself out of trouble; nor do they bother to hide their feelings from their customers and other outsiders – thus leading to even lower sales, profitability and job security.

This is a vicious spiral and one that is not likely to have a happy ending. The worse the situation gets, the worse communication becomes. The worse communication becomes, the worse the financial situation gets. This is partly because nobody really cares, nobody really believes there is a future for the business anyway so there is little or no effort being spent to try to suggest ways in which it could be improved.

Ambassadors

We have already touched on the ambassadorial role of employees; without repeating all the facts here, it is worth reminding ourselves of the worth of this benefit. Nobody can ever be as good an ambassador for an organisation than the people who comprise it. Whether in the public or private sector, our first impression of that organisation is made by the people we encounter who work for it.

A major engineering company, which sells directly into both commercial and private customers, spends an absolute fortune on its image, customer service standards and quality standards, technical standards and everything else in life. Unfortunately, all that good work, and hard cash measured well into the tens of millions, can go down the drain when a service engineer calls. Overalls missing, dirty or scruffy, an attitude of not caring about the fault in the machinery or about his or her service levels, and the customer's opinion of the organisation are compounded as soon as he/she starts running down that organisation.

We've all heard it; it usually goes along the lines of "I don't know how many of these things I'm going to have to put right before 'they' realise that this kit is a load of crap. I've had so many call outs its perfectly obvious that the things are not right. They don't work, they're worse than what we had before and I hate to think what its costing the firm. But nobody will listen to me. Perhaps if they came out here they could explain to you why this is always going wrong, but I can't. All I can do is tell you that I can do something about it today but it'll probably be as bad tomorrow. You'd best put the kettle on; I'll be seeing you again soon."

Far from being fanciful, that is almost a verbatim transcript of the utterings of a senior service engineer who called at our office a short time ago. If he repeated even a small part of that to even a small part of his customer base, it's hardly surprising that many customers are now choosing to shop elsewhere.

Incidentally, you'll notice that it's never his fault; it's always the responsibility of somebody else. While that side of human nature can probably never be eradicated, it could be alleviated by better communication. Even if a representative like this hardly ever sees head office, which he doesn't, a better level of communication would at least help him to understand why the things go wrong, what to do about it, what the firm is doing about it and what to say (and what not to say) to his customers. And this is a multi-million pound business, not a small drinks company.

Better communication too would help to enrich this particular employees' lifestyle. It can't be much fun going around complaining about your own employer. At the very least you lose self-respect because you wonder what on earth you're doing working for such a bad outfit. Feeling better about yourself is one of the most positive aspects that good communications can bring to bear on the life of an employee. The working lifestyle is hard enough for most of us as it is without it being made harder by a singular lack of two-way communication. It can be made easier by the knowledge that somebody is listening to what you say, maybe even acting on it and that, therefore, there is a caring face to the organisation which, maybe, you hadn't suspected. If none of these beliefs are in place it is not surprising that an employee is demotivated.

Empowerment and Belonging

Empowerment is, of course, about much more than internal communications, but a strong sense of belonging brought about by open and honest communications can help greatly. Certainly, being kept in the dark and fed on manure is not the kind of enrichment that is conducive to developing human employees, despite the enrichment it might bring to mushrooms.

Finally, this sense of belonging to an organisation is important. Taking the EU definition, which has been approved by the Council of Ministers, 'exclusion' is one of the key aspects of poverty and deprivation in our society: the exclusion from taking part in society because of a lack of means to do so. Poor internal communications is simply an extension of that argument. By excluding employees from information, an organisation, which communicates poorly, is effectively excluding them from its own society. They do not know how to take part, where or when or even whether they'll be welcome if they try. Not surprisingly they turn elsewhere for their activities and their job becomes, and remains, a meal ticket, there to be done to pay the bills until something better comes along.

This attitude, too, will never be eradicated, but it can be reduced by making people feel that they are part of their organisation – an important, if minor, part. Telling them what it is all about is a good start to this process. Telling them how they fit into it is an even better development. Telling them how they could make it even better is the logical conclusion.

So, what is the broad message likely to be in most situations? This is not as simple a question as it may seem. The answer can be fairly simplistic, it can embrace all kinds of good news: financial results, successful achievements of various kinds, successful takeovers, mergers or joint ventures, new product or service launches and similar platforms for encouraging employees to look on the bright side of working with their organisation.

There is, for instance, little point in spending a fortune on launching a new product or service to the outside world unless it has been fully launched to employees first. To allow employees to read about it first in their local papers is not only a gross discourtesy, it is downright silly management. It ignores the potential of the ambassadorial role that we have looked at and the potential for those employees to sell the product or service as part of their normal social activities.

The value of this social sales effect can be overlooked. When the Austin Metro was first launched in October 1980, the Communications Manager of Austin Morris was invited to speak about it to the Birmingham branch of Soroptimist International (an association of professional women who hold regular dinner meetings). Out of a room of about 60 people, five decided to buy a Metro there and then and a further three subsequently placed orders within a couple of weeks. Selling eight new cars in one evening is not a bad bit of icing on the cake of the normal process of sales and marketing.

Employees can also sometimes spot a flaw in either the new offering or the way in which it is being launched which could be embarrassing if it reaches the external world without being corrected. Sometimes they have inside knowledge of the product or service that is not shared by the marketing function – especially if external agencies have played a large part in the launch planning and strategy.

Since employees often know quite a lot about a new product or service anyway, there are very few considerations of confidentiality to worry about. Quite the opposite; if a big launch campaign is about to break, the issue of secrecy is no longer valid and the more share of voice the debutante product receives, the better the overall reception is likely to be.

Incentives

Strong financial results are often quoted as being platforms from which companies can offer incentives and exhort employees to greater efforts, especially if there is a financial reward of some sort linked into those results for the employees. Interestingly, a number of latter day quality gurus, such as Ronnie Lessem, are preaching the wisdom of scrapping incentive schemes which are based on financial reward for greater effort. This way, the argument goes, greater heights can be scaled only spasmodically and this lack of consistency can harm quality – which relies on consistency above all else – rather than have the desired effect upon the organisation and the quality process.

From the purist quality crusader's point of view, there is merit in this. From the broader and human point of view, it is less valid and approaches pure cant. Unless employees are involved, they are not going to bother about quality of manufacture or service, they are not going to go the extra mile in helping colleagues to cope with their difficulties and they are certainly not going to embrace concepts such as partnering with anything approaching enthusiasm.

If Karl Marx achieved nothing else, he at least managed to get across the need for shared ownership of the resources, responsibility, success and rewards of what he called the capitalist entity. That message is no less valid today; probably even more valid than in his mid-19th century, since levels of education have risen so widely and since the majority of the population is now enfranchised in an economic as well as a political sense.

Employees must have a financial incentive to try their hardest, which is why, in many cases, the public sector finds it so difficult to motivate its employees. Ultimately, the co-operative is a very attractive form of organisational structure. The main problem with it is that it falls down when human nature is taken into account. What works well on paper tends not to translate too easily to practical implementation; again partnering is a good case in point. It looks fine to accept communal responsibility for difficult issues until you realise that those issues may affect you, your professional and personal reputation. They may affect the performance of your organisation and the financial success or otherwise of the project as a whole, and that could affect your own bottom line. Then it all begins to look much more difficult and the temptation to allocate blame elsewhere is likely to re-surface.

So it is with employee communications. Take a short extract from Ronnie Lessem's book *Total Quality Learning* in which he is exhorting managers to apply skills in the area of innovation.

Involving people.

- How do you effect shared values whereby people will co-operate with you in your application of a particular skill?
- How do you ensure that whatever skill you apply is accessible to the people with whom you work?
- How do you keep things eminently practical?
- How do you keep people enthusiastic?

The answer to this last question would be illuminating but sadly, he does not venture to voice it.

Finally, and ultimately, the originally envisaged skills need to be embodied in a simple tangible form in order to inspire effort.

- How do you keep your people's energy level from waning, in relation to the skill being implemented?
- How do you impose a sense of urgency?
- How do you maintain a bias for action?

It would be useful to quote the answers to these questions as well, but Mr Lessem has not provided them. Nevertheless, there are interesting questions here in terms of internal communications, not least the point about imposing a sense of urgency. What better way than to spell out the consequences if achievement is wildly adrift of target? That could have as strong an effect on quality achievement as most of the quality gurus' dictats put together.

This is the kind of message commonly communicated in internal marketing cultures, together with the usual strictures about continuing to support the functions to which your own department provides a service; and there is nothing wrong with that. Indeed, if a few more organisations practised it, the national economy might flourish a little more.

Bad News

But news isn't always good, especially in what appears to be a roller coaster ride of economic boom one minute and gloom the next. Ironically, the very time when internal communications really comes into its own is when an organisation has bad news to impart – redundancies, short-time working, closures, streamlining and so on.

This is the very moment that employees need to be able to trust their organisation and want their employers to tell them exactly what is going on, why and what the implications are for them. This is a time of anxiety, uncertainty, possible redundancy and general insecurity, which is very understandable. Unfortunately, this need often comes at the worst time for management who may, themselves, not know exactly what is going on, especially if the organisation is multinational and who may share those uncertainties and fears for their own security.

There was a classic case of this recently when a US-owned multinational embarked upon a streamlining – or downsizing, rightsizing or simple cost-cutting – exercise which involved employees all over the world. The US-based management remembered to tell most of the offices about the proposed cuts – but not quite all. Those in at least three territories found out either from the jungle telegraph rumour machine within the organisation or from their local media.

Mistakes do, of course, occur but this is a particularly unfortunate one. It was made more so by the fact that the three territories in question were in Asia, where sensitivities over what can too easily be viewed as US economic imperialism are already present. This kind of oversight makes mistakes even more likely to occur. The vicious spiral continues with the perception that the organisation adopted an uncaring attitude to those particular employees because not only were they not American, but they were Asian.

On a smaller scale, in the early-1990s, a British industrial concern had over-reached itself financially and was forced to scale down. The job losses were not, in fact, very great and were confined to voluntary redundancy with the exception of one plant. When asked how he was going to communicate it, the Managing Director replied with a cheery "Oh, that's all right; we'll just do it." As it turned out, they didn't do it, because, on their own subsequent admission, they all thought that somebody else was going to do it and had not planned for a comprehensive communications exercise.

To make matters worse, the plant that had been forgotten was in Northern Ireland, a sensitive area at the best of times. Because it had been left too late, the exercise ended up costing him far more than it would have done had Northern Ireland been covered with the rest of the UK, although he was of the opinion that it was a small price to pay for the relative ease of mind which a professional job finally brought.

A third example from 1998 serves to underline the point. A major financial company prided itself on having launched a new newsletter for staff which had been pretty well received and had undoubtedly filled a gap in internal communications, even though some of it was probably taken with a pinch of salt.

Then the reorganisation started; the usual thing, voluntary redundancies were called for to shed 20 per cent of the staff (around 6,000 people altogether). In all the excitement of the restructuring and all the uncertainty of who was going to be asked to volunteer (because many volunteers need to have the principle suggested to them), everyone forgot all about the newsletter which not only did not address the very issue that employees were concerned about but did not even appear in its regular slot a week or two after the rumours started.

This is doubly unfortunate. Here was a good communications platform that, although it had its faults, was at least known by employees and reckoned to be accurate as far as it went. Yet the very first time that it was really needed to put a gloss of truth and reassurance on the uncertainty, it failed in that task and effectively committed suicide. Never again is it likely to retain the trust of a workforce which it has let down over a key issue. Even if the managers responsible for getting it out had not survived the reorganisation, the newsletter could have delivered as accurate and constructive a picture of the situation as was possible. Even if it had only confirmed rumour and told employees where and how to volunteer, it would have had a clarifying role. As it happened, it could have done a great deal more than that and actually helped to channel frustrations and emotions into a much more positive mode than was actually the case.

It is too easy to forget that there are communications systems that are ready and able to disseminate information of this nature once bad news arises. In the last example, there was a very competent internal communications function headed by a very able manager who was tearing out her hair because her services with their attendant benefits of fast, accurate and credible communications channels were being ignored. Sometimes, in extreme circumstances, it is possible that senior managers might mistrust an internal communications function and wish to bypass it.

Or they might believe, rightly in some cases, that this is a job which only senior management itself can undertake and arrange a series of presentations or other communications exercises accordingly. However, in this case, the very existence of the function seems to have been overlooked. It is strange that a facility which has cost a good deal of senior management time, effort and resource should be overlooked at the very time at which it could prove most fruitful, but it clearly does happen.

Proving the Benefits

Nevertheless, it could be argued that it is up to the internal communications function to prove itself in such circumstances, especially in the processes of change management, so that they cannot be overlooked. One of the more perceptive senior managers at Saatchis used to remark that the essence of a good consultancy was to make itself indispensable to the client. In the same way an internal communications function needs to be constantly proving its worth – more so than many other functions – in order to be remembered at a time of excitement or in a crisis.

Sometimes, this can be done largely on personality. Sometimes, it has to be carried out in a more considered and measured way, which clearly links benefits to investment. This is not easy, and we shall look at evaluation techniques in a later chapter, but sometimes a snap shot health check or a quick attitude survey can provide a treasure chest of data which senior managers find it hard to ignore – certainly harder than the clamourings of a handful of middle managers.

Indeed, a great deal of change management (to use the fashionable parlance) consists of good, timely and accurate internal communications. The major difficulty is usually not so much the ability and willingness to inform the employees as a whole but the ability and willingness of senior management to release the facts to the internal communications function. There is still the viewpoint in the minds of many managers that knowledge is power and that, if they share that knowledge with more junior staff, they will, in some mysterious way, be eroding part of their own power.

Yet what is knowledge but facts which may change within a few hours? There is seldom any great mystique about it, rather a question of timing and sensitivity of the type and nature of the information-imparting process. Of course, it is one thing to write this in a book; it is another thing altogether to assess the level and timing of the release of highly sensitive information in circumstances when the livelihoods of many employees may be at stake.

That notwithstanding, the whole process of change is one that necessitates securing the support of as many employees as possible. Without this support, the whole change process could either fail or be made a great deal harder to push through; if done so against the wishes of an organised and informed set of employees.

However, we must also remember the dictum in an earlier chapter that communications, whether for change or for other purposes, is a two-way process. And two-way processes need to be thought out rather more carefully in advance than mere 'seat of the pants' communications.

For a start, they need to be carefully planned, a process which we shall explore in the following chapters. This planning process has to take into account the ability and opportunity of employees to carry on a dialogue about the topics in question. It doesn't have to degenerate into an argy bargy, just a facility for them to air their views over what might be a very sensitive issue. New and improving technology enables this process to happen much more regularly and easily now than used to be the case even ten years ago. Then it was all about mass meetings, cascade and reverse cascade groups and the laborious process of letters to newsletters, few of which ever got printed within a couple of months of the original airing of the topic, by which time most people had forgotten what on earth it was all about.

Now e-mail, intranets, video conferencing and all the rest of the modern facilities make this process much easier. Like windscreen washers, you wonder what people ever did before they were invented, but these gadgets also bring with them a new managerial responsibility to be able to respond to the response. One of the great assets of these new technologies is their immediacy. A message can be placed on e-mail and replied to within minutes. Not only that, it can be copied all over a huge organisation, globally if necessary, so that not only the originator but the rest of the workforce can be let into the debate. Clearly, this can get out of hand if sensible controls are not applied.

One way is to request that all responses are funnelled through the section head; sometimes this works, depending on the attitude and managerial abilities of the section head.

Another way is to place only some of the original information on e-mail and keep the rest up your sleeve for the inevitable requests for further enlightenment. It just may be that there is too little interest to force the rest of the information out into the organisational domain. This is not an ideal method of communicating internally, as it obviously has a number of faults – lack of complete honesty being one of them – but it has been used *in extremis* by a management keen to involve a workforce without handing over the initiative.

More constructive is the relatively old-fashioned method of calling a series of team briefings or sectional presentations at a prearranged place and time and releasing the information simultaneously. This prevents organised resistance, at least to start with. It also allows all concerned to see the colour of each other's eyes – a necessity in clear and honest communications – and it allows a reasonable right of reply without incurring the risks of debate by e-mail.

Human Contact

Old fashioned it may be, but nobody has yet replaced human contact as the ideal communications tool. It is, after all, all about people and not machines. Even a company as technologically advanced as BT still holds regular meetings for its top managers as being the best way of keeping them informed about what is going on than to allow too much information to leak out on e-mails and other processes. The trouble is that once the information is out on the network, it is very difficult to control or safeguard. Security of various information systems is currently one of the banes of the developed world and no breakthrough has yet suggested that the problem is solved. Until it is, the need for relative confidentiality is paramount and dictates the need to continue with apparently old-fashioned and costly, but still very practical, methods.

Furthermore, the right of reply should follow the normal bottom up process of communicating through natural line managers. Again we see the importance of the line manager role; here as one who can receive, gather and collate reaction to an issue from his or her employees as well as one who is charged with imparting that knowledge in the first place. All the more reason to train line managers properly.

If this bottom up process is put in place and made to work – and it will not work of its own accord or without a good deal of investment in time and effort – then it is one of the best ways in which an organisation can truly involve its employees, especially at key moments like times of change.

It cannot work without the communications culture being put in place; perversely the communications culture cannot simply be injected like a dose of medicine. The culture has to be carefully nurtured, planned and developed in order to allow employees the confidence and the freedom with which to take advantage of systems that give them a feedback role. Culture without systems and vice versa are recipes for something between a disaster and a half-baked solution, neither of which is going to be particularly effective.

External Aspects

There are, of course, a number of external aspects to the conceptual approach to internal communications. It is fairly easy to tell an organisation in which the practice is well established, for example. It is even easier and more depressing to tell an organisation in which internal communications is either embryonic or non-existent. Both ends of this spectrum and the various shades of grey in between can tell a great deal about the organisation to the external observer.

For instance, if the employees encountered are knowledgeable, confident about the policies and products or services of the organisation, if they know where to go to get answers rapidly, if they can explain how something has happened, then they probably have a strong grasp of what their employer is all about. In this case, they are likely to be fortunate enough, or perceptive enough, to work for an organisation which is enlightened enough to bring them into the mainstream of its culture and to keep telling them what is happening and why.

If, on the other hand, the employee encountered knows very little about his/her role, who to contact for help, cannot explain why something is not right, has no idea what the organisation's policies are and doesn't seem to care either, then he/she may well be a product of faulty internal communication.

The former British Rail used to be a case in point. Very few members of staff ever seemed to know why a train was running late, when it would arrive, whether the next one was on time or what was the cause of all this chaos. For customers, that could easily become extremely annoying, as so many opinion polls about the levels of customer satisfaction showed. In theory, the position has improved and, indeed, there is more information now available through the new train operating companies about what is happening and why; there are even apologies from time to time. With even better internal communications, however, there might be less need for apologies.

Important issues about management also come over to the public in ways which are sometimes unexpected, again showing the need for careful communications internally which are going to be reflected in the utterances of organisational spokespeople. For example, the former motor racing World Champion, Damon Hill was interviewed by *The Times* on 30 May 1998 about his then new team, Jordan. Part of his answer is very revealing:

It [success] is about being clinically accurate . . . and understanding the level of work and the standard that we are going to have to achieve. But it is a management job, part of Eddie's [Jordan] job, to look at how the team can be injected with these higher standards and a better understanding, without upsetting the balance.

A perfectly cogent, considered quotation which reveals a good deal not just about team strategy and the difficulties in which Jordan found itself – with, basically, an uncompetitive engine – but also about the way in which the team communicates within itself. Hill's perception was that the onus for leading towards these higher standards lay with Jordan. The implication is that this is not understood by everyone involved, possibly even Jordan himself. The resulting impression on the part of the reader is of a team which has not sorted out exactly who is doing what, to whom, why, how and by when. Consequently, Hill's failure to score any points in the previous six races comes as no surprise. Yet Hill is an excellent ambassador and one in whom most team chiefs would gladly put their trust.

Corporate Image

So, a strong internal communications policy vigorously pursued can lead to a greater confidence in the organisation on the part of external observers. This, in itself, is enough to justify the policy to many senior managers, especially those who realise the value of a strong corporate image for their organisations. Oddly, not all senior managers do realise this value. When they don't, they tend to rely on other factors and decisions to make their impact: pricing, customer service, cost efficiency, acquisitions, investment in new systems, diversification and so on. What is too often overlooked is that all of these decisions automatically have an impact upon the corporate image of their organisations, whether the managers like it or not. They are going to be seen and interpreted by industry sector observers, including customers, analysts and the media, as being symptomatic of the health of the organisation.

Observers also look at the way in which the organisation comes across through its employees; what is an organisation but its employees anyway? Even the chairman or CEO is often an employee. Every hint they give about what is going on within the organisation is analysed and combed for further enlightenment, especially in financial circles. Whether the senior management team has confidence in its future can decide whether the City has the confidence to invest and recommend investment in the organisation's future. Thus, how those managers, as employees, are presented to the external world is critical to the confidence of that world in that organisation.

Employees do not have to be in junior posts to feel they are not being communicated with properly. Many middle and senior managers also feel the same way – and that is dangerous. By representing their employer, they are in a position of influence and any weakness they show in the confidence they have in their organisation can lead to a corresponding weakness in the confidence of observers. The Damon Hill example proves this too; not many managers are paid £4.5 million (plus a fast car with only one careful driver) and his views on internal communications within the Jordan team are likely to contribute strongly to the impression formed of that team by others.

Bluff and counter bluff can be a part of the game when a competitor is known to be carrying out scrutiny. It could be that Hill was deliberately trying to lead the rest of the F1 teams up the garden path by giving them a false impression of lack of teamwork at Jordan. Given the set of results that Jordan had achieved in the 1998 season, however, this is unlikely. Sport, like investment and business success, is about confidence, not dissembling.

Knowledge as Power

As we have seen, not all senior managers share this view that internal communications is key to the performance of their organisation. Most will pay lip service to it without actually condemning it, but there is still the feeling that knowledge is power that cannot be shared without a weakening of one's own personal power base. Insecurity will never be eradicated and it is likely to take more than one book to change the attitudes of the chronically paranoid strata of senior management which are so evident in some organisations.

There is, for instance, a local government authority whose CEO briefed the senior management team – effectively, the heads of departments – on a particularly important issue in the throes of local government reorganisation in the mid-1990s. There was even a lengthy (and semi-intelligible) memo produced from the CEO's office that sought to put the point of view of the council on the thorny issue – although it probably reflected the views of the management team rather than those of the elected councillors. The instruction with it was to communicate it to all staff at the discretion of the team leaders.

Several weeks later, many departments had never heard of this memo, did not know what stance the council was taking about the issue, did not even know that their heads had had a formal briefing session with the CEO. Anxiety, rumour, lack of confidence in managers and a desire to find another, safer bolthole were paramount. When most employees finally found out what their council thought, it was through the pages of the local newspaper with an inevitable overlay of interpretation which did not necessarily reflect very accurately the views of senior managers or councillors. It is depressingly likely that this is not an isolated example but rather is symptomatic of the fears and reservations of many senior managers in many walks of life.

Finance people seem to be particularly suspicious. Perhaps it's because they deal in caution, hard figures and difficult budget balancing acts and find it sometimes hard to explain much of what they do to a, relatively, innumerate

audience. Perhaps it's also because the real financial position of many organisations would, if revealed publicly (which is always an inherent risk of
internal communications) frighten existing and potential investors witless.
Perhaps it's just an awkwardness with words and presentation techniques
which makes them shy away from it.

Nevertheless the financial area is one which is most critical to the success
of any internal communication exercise. If the financial background to the
organisation is not properly explained, many misapprehensions are likely to
follow – and some of them may turn out to be well-founded.

So, ultimately, the concept of powerful internal communications is about
power sharing: the sharing of information with employees so that they are
more enlightened about their organisation. It takes courage and integrity to
be prepared to share power. Internal communications is one measure of that
courage and integrity.

CHAPTER SIX

Planning

More time has been wasted in management terms by a lack of planning than by almost any other failing. Doing the job is relatively simple – once it has been planned. The old saying that any fool can do the job but it takes brains to plan it is nowhere more evident than in internal communications.

Planning performs a number of useful tasks, not all of them immediately evident. First, it sets the ground rules. What can and, equally important, what cannot be achieved? What needs to be done by when? Who is going to do it? How and where it will take place? All these are very relevant questions in any internal communications exercise.

First, what do we mean by planning? It's a bit like what do we mean by love? There are whole books written about the subject, which makes it even harder to understand why so few managers bother with it, and they sometimes cloak the topic in a pall of mystique which doesn't serve anyone particularly well.

In internal communications terms, planning is usually applied to the overall campaign, a network of activities over a given timescale, aimed at achieving given objectives. There will always be a strategic element, or there should be, and there is often a financial element as well. There are many planning models, a lot of them having been tried and tested in the fire of real-life experience. Most of these will be useful and your own organisational management may have a particular preference for the way in which they want to see the plans worked out.

However, the following pattern is one that has stood the test of most internal communications needs over the last twenty years and it may be useful as a starter or as a developmental device.

Research

The first stage is to carry out as much research as possible without offending anybody. This sounds self-evident, but sometimes, it seems as though not enough research is carried out within organisations. Again, there is a clear parallel with external marketing practice. Very few new products would be launched on to a completely cold marketplace without some parameters of market intelligence having first been drawn up; usually this will have been carried out through some form of research. Often the research will have been extensive, detailed, costly and very carefully structured. So it should be internally.

There are occasions when internal research can, in itself, satisfy some of the needs of the internal audience. The very fact that employees see it being carried out, that they are asked to take part, that they are asked to contribute their opinion can be very useful. For them it is a cathartic experience – if carried out sensitively and carefully. It means that somebody in management values their opinion enough to canvas it. It means that they might be listened to, that their feelings matter and that their voice can be heard.

There is also, of course, the fact that it will almost certainly reveal a good deal about the feelings of the employees and their attitudes to their employer. Some of this information may have known by management before the research; much of it probably will not have been. At its best, it will comprise a treasure chest of knowledge that can be used for all sorts of purposes, not just for planning the rest of the internal communications activities.

There may, for instance, be localised but very useful knowledge about the workings of a particular department, process, management team or unit. This may shed light on an issue which has been puzzling management for some time; it may help to explain why something which should have worked has not. For example, in the 1980s, a large marketing company decided to join in the computer revolution and install computer systems which gave all employees (about 90 people) their own work stations. Nothing odd about that; everyone was doing it at the time and it was merely keeping up with the trend.

However, after a few weeks it became clear that it simply wasn't working. Not that the computer systems were always crashing – although there was a lot of down time in the early days – or that they were incapable of doing what they were there to do, which was largely wordprocessing and spreadsheet work. Reports failed to arrive in time, creative work was late, badly bodged or non-existent and the pressure on secretaries to get documents typed out was stronger rather than lessened.

A mini-survey was planned and carried out at the request of the board. It was completed not by the managers themselves but by the computer company which had provided and installed the system and which had also trained the staff. It sent two of its trainers into the offices and talked to all the 90 people involved. The answer proved to be blindingly simple but it was one that the board had never suspected. Apart from the secretaries, almost all the female staff working in the office – roughly two thirds of the total – were strongly resistant to using the new work stations. In fact they were so resistant that some had even unplugged the equipment, taken it off the desk and left it on the floor in a corner. The reason? If they were seen to be working at a keyboard, everyone would think that they were typists or secretaries and that offended their sense of self-esteem.

That proved to be a totally unsuspected but very thorny problem. Some of the women concerned were extremely prickly about their status and were adamant that the new system was not going to work. Further, they were going to ensure that it did not. Even the board of directors (half of whom were also women) was taken aback by this – and those directors thought they had seen just about everything. The solution proved long and costly – more training, more introduction to the benefits of the system, more men being seen to be writing their own reports and documents on the terminals. Even the Luddite chairman whose technical expertise began and stopped at a screwdriver, was persuaded to have one on his desk, although whether he ever actually used it is open to doubt. But for that piece of research, the agency might still be creating all its work with quill pens by the light of a rush taper.

Consequently, the internal audit is a very useful starting point but, like most activities, it has to be planned properly. First, what do you need to know? Employees' viewpoints in general are not a tight enough objective to act as a working brief. The remit has to be about a specific aspect of their opinions – a new way of working, a new building, a new structure, a new product or service, a reorganisation, a change in the way in which the organisation does things. Consequently, the questionnaire needs to be written from a specific viewpoint that starts from a specific, tightly defined basis and works towards a broader level of opinion. For example, the first questions might relate to specific changes or situations, move on to employees' views on these, then broaden out to related issues and finally end with an all embracing question.

One of the most useful examples of an attitude survey is the following questionnaire that was developed for, and put into practice with, a leading local government body in the 1990s. It was the basis for a face to face discussion between an interviewer and 32 senior managers within the organisation and all the data was then collated, analysed and presented back to that group of managers with a number of recommendations about how internal communications could be improved. The major criticism that can be levelled at this exercise is that it involved only heads of departments; opinions were not sought from those employees at whom the communications were aimed.

The result was a slow but unmistakable shift in the way in which that authority decided to communicate within itself. It certainly did not become perfect overnight, and there is still much work to do, but it did give itself a chance to escape from the 19th century, which is where most of its critics described it as being positioned before the exercise and its recommendations took place.

To quote verbatim:

Introduction

This exercise will investigate the current provision of internal communications facilities throughout the organisation and present a factual report to the director of PR. It will not attempt to evaluate any of the facilities at this stage; neither will it canvas staff views on any issue affecting internal communications.

This is, of course, a nonsense. What the survey really needed to do was to evaluate all the facilities and, even more importantly, to evaluate the attitudes of the managers and staff towards internal communications. However, it was precisely because these attitudes were suspected to be so prickly, and because it was felt by the commissioning manager that any attempt to evaluate her colleagues would be perceived as an unwarranted attack on their professionalism (thus setting back the cause of open internal communication for several more decades), that the survey was so restricted. Despite this, it managed to reveal a great deal about the way in which those managers went about the task of communicating. The introduction continued:

> The exercise will be conducted through personal discussion and visits to the departments involved. In order to ensure consistency between each area, a basic framework of criteria will be used in all cases. The basis of these criteria is set out below.

Areas of Enquiry

1.0 Facilities

1.1 Are there notice boards in the department? [This is a fairly basic question with a closed Yes/No tick box. Generally this question lulls respondents into a sense of security although, in this instance, not everyone said there were notice boards.]

1.2 If so, how many? [Answers ranged from 1 to 30.]

1.3 How visible are they? [To make it easier to evaluate, answers were grouped into three categories: 'impossible to miss', 'in a major traffic area' or 'easy to avoid'.]

1.4 Are they regularly used by those wishing to put up notices? [Again, a straight Yes/No tick box.]

1.5 Are they available for general use or restricted to certain types of information from certain sources? [Answers were grouped into the four categories of 'general use', 'use with permission', 'restricted' or 'both restricted and general'.]

1.6 Are they widely read? [Answers were again grouped into 'read by 100 per cent of staff', 'over 80 per cent', '50-80 per cent' and 'less than 50 per cent'.]

This first section was quickly and easily completed and had the effect of relaxing managers so that they began to feel less threatened. At this point, they also usually begin to believe that all the subject matter is going to be easily answered without casting doubts on their abilities as communicators.

So, as well as providing useful, if elementary, information, the first section settles down the managers and makes them more receptive to the concept of the assisted questionnaire. The second section became a little more ambitious.

2.0 Printed material

2.1 Do members of staff regularly receive departmental newsletters, magazines, or any other types of internal document? [Answers included the usual newsletters or magazines.]

2.2 If so, how are they obtained or delivered? [The hidden agenda here was that the centrally created documents did not seem to be reaching staff and there were suspicions – reasonably well founded as it turned out – that some of the departmental managers were either not bothering to have them distributed or else were deliberately suppressing them. The answers showed that this was indeed the case in a minority of departments.]

2.3 Are they generally read by those who receive them? [Again, a quantifiable range of answers was available: '100 per cent', '75-100 per cent', '50-75 per cent' '25-50 per cent' and 'less than 25 per cent'.]

2.4 Do the readers have any opportunity to contribute their own input to these document? [Answers here are 'yes', 'sometimes' or 'no'.]

2.5 Do staff receive briefing memos or similar documents from senior managers? [The boxes of 'yes', 'sometimes' and 'no' were repeated.]

2.6 If so, do these memos deal with specific issues or with general news of the organisation? [With three tick boxes for these two categories allowing multiple choice answers.]

This section cleared away a lot of confusion about whether staff were receiving the written documents that central management thought they were – or should be receiving. Without wishing to give away any secrets, in many internal audits, the answers are often very much less than 100 per cent, as they were in this example.

The next section began to look at the hub of the issues and deliberately strayed into the really thorny area.

3.0 Management involvement

3.1 Do managers ever give briefings to all or part of a department? [With tick boxes for 'regularly', 'sometimes' and 'never'.]

3.2 On what sort of topics? ['Corporate', 'departmental' or 'other'. This begins to sort out the managers who are committed to corporate, as opposed to departmental, internal communications.]

3.3 Is attendance compulsory? ['Always', 'sometimes', 'never'. If it isn't, of course, there is little point in holding the briefing in the first place.]

3.4 Do they take place during working hours? ['Yes', 'sometimes', 'never'.]

3.5 Is there a 'leave-behind' document? ['Always', 'sometimes', 'never'. Most memories are comparatively short and most employees need a reminder in the form of a piece of print that they can refer to and discuss with their families.]

3.6 Do the presenters use visual aids? ['Always', 'sometimes', 'never'. If they don't, they have just twelve minutes in which to deliver their message before the audience attention strays; few managers are this good at presentation and communication.]

3.7 How professional is the delivery? ['Excellent', 'good', 'adequate', 'poor'. This is, of course, a subjective assessment but, then, audiences, especially internal ones, are subjective.]

3.8 Is there an opportunity to reply from the floor? ['Always', 'sometimes', 'never'. If not, the briefing is often a waste of time and effort.]

3.9 Are there ever management briefing sessions confined to middle managers? ['Often', 'rarely'. A perfectly legitimate approach to internal communications provided the information is useful to middle management.]

3.10 Where are these held? ['Internally', 'externally'. Beware the seduction of expensive management away-days; they can cause resentment in other employee areas.]

3.11 What sort of topics do they address? ['Corporate', 'departmental'. Ideally, they should be both, but that is not very common.]

This section effectively sorted out the sheep from the goats by bringing the whole managerial commitment under the microscope. Yet most managers are happy to answer this sort of question – unless they have something very serious to hide. Many try to create positive answers on the spot and then follow up later; unfortunately, most fall down on the follow up process. Next, and very importantly, the questionnaire looks at the input of the corporate communications functions.

4.0 Corporate communications

4.1 Does the department ever receive internal communications in the form of written material from the organisation? ['Regularly', 'rarely'. "If not, why not?" seems to be a supplementary question here, but it might be unwise if it were included.]

4.2 Is there an opportunity to reply to a document? ['Always', 'sometimes', 'never'.]

4.3 Do corporate managers ever visit the department to meet staff and bring themselves up to date with developments? ['Regularly', 'sometimes', 'never'. If they don't, they can hardly be perceived as corporate managers.]

This is the basic test of how effective a corporate communications function is and can of course be greatly extended – as can all these points. However, for a first stab at getting towards the truth it is often enough to see whether the central function is on the right track.

Finally, the questionnaire looks at the real issues, now that the managers have congratulated themselves on surviving so far.

5.0 General

5.1 Is the department kept well informed about what is going on the organisation?

5.2 If not, what other information would be useful ?

5.3 Could any specific improvement be made in internal communications?

Much of the value of this questionnaire comes in this last section, which often gives rise to some highly creative and very relevant ideas. The snag sometimes comes in getting those ideas accepted and put into practice.

Objectives

After research, the next major planning task is setting the objectives. This sounds easy and, sometimes, it is. Clearly, without objectives there is a greatly reduced chance of achieving anything worthwhile – and an even greater chance of taking the eye off the ball so that a great deal of effort can sometimes produce very little tangible outcome.

For the purposes of internal communications, or internal marketing, the objectives are very similar to those of external communications or external marketing. If this were a treatise on planning an FMCG (fast moving consumer goods) campaign, the objectives would probably look something like numerical targets. Usually they would be set out in quantitative terms, because only then can performance be properly measured and monitored.

In *The Basic Art of Marketing*, Ray Willsmer sets out a typical marketing objective:

> A simple statement such as to have 15 per cent of the market and a profit of £50,000 next year but 50 per cent and £350,000 within five years. This gives an important indication of strategy to the reviewing manager who, otherwise, might regard it as a minor brand with few pretences.

Neatly put. And the thinking can be transferred very simply to the planning of the internal communications campaign by setting quantifiable objectives for the coming year, or campaign, in particular and for the future three years in more general terms. It is also important to state in as precise and measurable a way as possible what exactly is involved in these objectives.

In order to help with this, many good internal communications practitioners will set SMART objectives. Old friends to those with management training, SMART objectives nevertheless are more than a hackneyed way of bamboozling junior, or even senior, managers; they can be extremely useful in determining exactly what it is that you need to achieve. The system is quite simple. Objectives should be:

- specific;

- measurable;

- attainable;

- realistic;

- timed.

No great mystique there, but a sensible and practical guide to what to write into objectives.

Looking at it in more detail, the overall objectives must be *specific*. In other words, a particular target needs to be identified. Perhaps it is a better understanding among employees of a particular management strategy or marketing campaign; perhaps it is an acceptance of new working practices, or perhaps it is an increase in productivity. All these things can be measured in some form and they are all, therefore, specific.

Measurement is just as important in internal campaigns as in external ones and this is why the objectives must be capable of being measured against a quantitative basis. Thus, it is necessary to get a message across to a certain number of employees by a certain time, or to be able to measure the strength and depth of knowledge about an issue as a result of the communications campaign. Measurement is often greatly helped by an audit.

Attainable objectives are important. There is no point in setting a target that nobody has a realistic chance of achieving, like a latter day Holy Grail. That just demotivates staff, who think that there is little point in trying if they are never going to be able to achieve anything – and they may have a point.

By the same token, *realistic* means that objectives have to be based in reality, to be tangible, achievable goals rather than vague motherhood statements such as some mission statements tend to be. There is a striking example of a mission statement used by a major international leisure chain that never fails to draw gasps of horror from delegates when used in training. It reads:

> To be recognised as the market leader in service excellence by creating a continuous improvement process driven by our customers and delivered by a committed and professional team.

Wonderful. It can mean all things to all people or nothing to anybody. It doesn't tell you what the organisation does, to whom, why or how. It is totally nebulous and probably took a huge amount of management time and effort for no good purpose. Objectives that are written like this need to be avoided, no matter how alluring they may appear to be. A simple statement that can be understood by everyone in the organisation is of far greater use than a meaningless series of managerial clichés.

Finally, *timed*. All objectives have to have a deadline. We could all achieve most things if only we were allowed a couple of centuries in which to do it. Unfortunately, life isn't like that and we need to focus on what it is possible to achieve before we finally shuffle off this mortal coil. So, put end times and intermediate target dates into the objectives, and make sure people stick to them. Policing planning to ensure that the plan doesn't stay on a dusty shelf is almost as important as writing it in the first place.

So, the objectives are clear, simple, understandable and SMART. The next two stages are relatively easy.

Key Messages

Key messages are those facts or opinions which you would like the employees to know about. They may be about the organisation's structure, progress, successes, people, investment, local activities or they may be about the management's view of the market place or analysis of a broader issue. Irrespective, they are the ammunition that an internal communications practitioner needs to fire off to the employees.

They don't always have to be positive, although they should not be negative if it can possibly be avoided. They do have to be truthful, and that might mean that they have to be very realistic – not afraid of facing up to the less palatable truths of a situation as well as claiming the glory when it does happen. If they are not true, however, the employees will soon find out. Just as journalists and broadcasters are unlikely to be hoodwinked for long, so employees are even quicker to seize on an untruth and unmask it. And once unmasked, it is very difficult to regain the lost credibility that the incident will have destroyed in the minds of the employees.

No employee likes to think that he/she is the victim of a propaganda war – that is why so many internal newspapers are wide of the mark and fail in their purpose. Employees are thinking consumers of news about the organisation; if the planning process remembers that, it is likely to be that much more accurate, respectful and successful.

The type of information incorporated at this stage in the planning process is again neatly summarised in the Schering plan.

> Ensuring that staff have a clear understanding of the shared vision, the value of their department and how their own personal role and objectives contribute to the ongoing development and success of the company.

Not many organisations can honestly say that their employees even know what the vision is, let alone how they themselves can play an active and useful role in it. If the vision is not to be buried in a dusty file for its lifetime, this kind of communication is vital.

> Ensuring that staff have the information they need to do their jobs efficiently and effectively.

Another point which has been touched on before but is worth repeating, if only because some managers seem to imagine that, in the absence of clear briefing, employees somehow divine their roles and responsibilities through a process of osmosis. This might just be possible after a great deal of practice, but it is better not left to chance.

> Ensuring that staff receive regular briefings on the performance of the company.

This is necessary so that they can take a pride in its successes and share in its concerns, otherwise, they are never going to feel that sense of belonging without which all effort is limited to the subjective objective of "What's in it for me?"

Giving staff information on the reason for change.

This is the nub of the issue in many cases. There is a school of management that believes that employees are invisible and inaudible until it comes to a change in structure and then they will become both bellicose and devious. Perhaps that could be because nobody thought about involving them at any earlier stage in the management process.

If reasons for change are spelt out clearly and simply to employees, half the problems associated with change management are solved, because most of those problems are not about money, locations, legal contracts and management style. Complex though these aspects can be, they pale into simplicity alongside the real issue in change management, which is people and the attitude of those people to the proposed changes.

Encouraging a corporate spirit of openness and participation, with particular emphasis on spoken communication.

'*Openness and participation*' are not qualities that come to mind too often in the great management game. Yet they are the strongest cards in the pack if they are properly used. They are qualities that can harness the goodwill of employees; they can channel the combined energy of the workforce, but not if they are never used. And to be used they must be communicated.

A common mistake is to write too many key messages. Similar to a marketing plan, it is tempting to go on until all the paper is used up. Often, these are largely variations on the same key messages or themes reiterated in a way that seems to be fresher than the last time the point arose. This is doing nobody a service for the messages must sometime, somehow, be distilled into very clear and concise statements. The more verbiage which surrounds them from the start, the harder this process becomes.

It is far better, therefore, to create them in simple, clear terms from the outset (as Schering has largely done) so that the translation is as painless as possible. Humanity generally understands clarity and simplicity and generally does not understand, and therefore suspects, complexity. That is a basic tenet of good internal communications.

One last point about key messages. Very often, there is a downside to the message. Nothing is ever that simple that it does not have an obverse side to it and messages are no exception. If, for instance, the message is something as apparently straightforward as a restructuring announcement, there are many hidden minefields. If the new structure is going to be so good, why has it not been implemented before? Why, if the new team is so great, have they been doing something entirely different until now? Was the old team, of which many of the recipients of the message may have been an integral part for a long time, really so hopeless that all this change had to be brought about?

Even a new product or service has its problems. If it is the latest thing, what about all the thousands of obsolete versions which were also the latest thing last year but are now cluttering up the shelves of retail outlets all over the place?

Clearly some tactful way has to be found to position the new alongside the old as a seamless, natural and evolutionary progression without necessarily condemning the old, especially when the old forms a large part of the audience. And that brings us to the target audiences themselves – the next stage in the planning process.

Target Audiences

Target audiences are one of the more straightforward aspects of planning; they are, put simply, those to whom the messages have to be communicated. Nothing very complicated in that, except that it is easy to think that you know an audience when, in fact, there are sometimes many unknown factors which may govern the way in which the communications process is planned.

Audiences for an internal communications plan are, usually, the employees. But employees are seldom neatly packaged in one place or organised in one centralised form which makes communication easy. Divisions, functions, groups, subsidiaries, profit centres, and joint venture partner employees can all be very important; yet they may be very difficult to reach.

They could also include staff at retail networks that sell the organisation's product or service. They could almost include sister companies or organisations and certainly those who have vested interests in the future of the organisation – its pensioners.

Also, what about employees' families? Often they know little about the work that their partners carry out; equally, they will exert influence over him or her, which the organisation cannot exert, no matter how hard it tries. In terms of persuasion, therefore, they can often be as important as communicating with the employee direct, something we shall look at in a later chapter.

So, the target audiences begin to take on a more complex profile than simply 'the employees'. Some organisations don't even recognise the term 'employee' for instance; if you go to Mars in Slough, you won't find any 'employees', only 'associates'. Whether the people concerned appreciate being termed associates is a moot point, but there is very little, if any, reference in the media to industrial disputes at Mars, although that could also have something to do with high pay levels.

To term 'employees' as 'associates' is not, in itself, a major step forward and is the butt of a number of somewhat unkind jokes in the profession, not confined to Mars. What is more important is that the people, whatever they are called, are given the respect which they are due and are brought into the culture of company knowledge without which they can never have any sense of belonging. It doesn't matter what you call them; it matters hugely what and how you communicate with them.

Strategy

What also matters more than anything else in planning is the next stage: the strategy. Strategy is the single most important area; if this is wrong or missing, the rest of the plan is useless. Many communications plans exist which have, to all intents and purposes, no clear-cut strategy. Where this is the case the chances of achieving anything are pretty remote.

The strategy is the broad way in which the organisation is going to communicate the messages to the audiences in order to achieve the objectives. Thus it is a clear and simple summary of what has gone before. It is also a blueprint against which the activity, which will be set out in the next section, i.e. the methodology, will be planned, executed and evaluated.

Strategies are broad brush strokes, not detailed minutiae. They should paint a fresh swathe of thinking in coloured tones across the canvas of an organisation's culture. If they do this well, they are invaluable. If they do not, they have not been properly thought through.

Strategies also need to imbue the plan with the elements of creativity – 'magic' as some singularly conceited communications consultant once called it – which is going to act as a platform, a method of carrying out the task *and at the same time enhance the process*. This is not an easy task, and it usually requires both experience and imagination. It is the main difference between workaday communicators and inspired ones. Very rarely is it overtly present but, when it is, it leaps out as a shining beacon of inspiration.

So, the good strategy will do more than simply restate the basic communication process. It will also contain a plank of activity – a process, an association with other parties, a device of some sort, an acknowledgement of working processes, such as vesting responsibility for communicating with certain line managers. Or it will contain something else which will differentiate the new communications process from all the others that have gone before.

This last point can be a real problem. So often internal communicators have to grapple with the failures of their predecessors. Initiatives have been started and not seen through; internal newsletters are a very good example. The first one is easy – like the first novel. The subsequent ones struggle. In the face of this kind of inconsistent achievement, the strategy needs to deliver what it promises in unequivocal terms. This means that the strategy needs to be capable of evaluation against the objectives. Some kind of measurement must take place – whether that be by external audit or some other method. The strategy must therefore build in this type of safeguard in order to demonstrate that the will is there to see through the programme to its conclusion – or to keep it going as a permanent state of affairs.

Consequently, the good strategy will have clauses in it which spell out the fact that the communications effort will be continuous and will be evaluated. It is not a mission statement; it does not seek to blind with science or confusing management speak. Rather, it seeks to clarify and inject innovation.

Thus, in a plan for an organisation with a disparate series of locations, there may be a strategy which states that it will use e-mail combined with personal presentation and regular documents and that the effectiveness of these will be tested at reasonable, but not regular, intervals. Here is the combination of methods, which tells all concerned what needs to happen and cannot be interpreted in misleading ways. It also states that whatever happens will be monitored and evaluated and implies that corrective action may need to be taken on the basis of the evidence supplied by the evaluation.

Surprisingly, few strategies of this nature seem to exist. Many organisations were asked to supply assistance in compiling this book and virtually all willingly agreed to do so. When asked for a sample internal communications plan, only one or two managed to provide one, yet, if any of those organisations had been asked for a business plan or a finance plan or even a marketing plan, my desk would probably have been flooded with sheets of paper.

Below is an example of an internal communications plan that can act as a template for most, but not all, cases. It was prepared for a US-owned, multinational organisation in the automotive industry in 1997. The background was a falling off of business in certain market sectors and geographical markets which had led to a series of redundancies at locations all over the world, especially in Europe. This plan set out to address what is a fairly typical situation.

For reasons of confidentiality, the research element is excluded but it showed a rapidly reducing workforce with declining confidence in the group and great anxiety for their future security. Not surprisingly this had already led to a number of key staff having gone elsewhere of their own volition.

Objectives

1. To secure as high a level of employee commitment as possible in [the organisation] in all territories within the next twelve months.

2. To empower staff to provide innovative solutions to the organisation's issues at every opportunity.

3. To ensure that all employees are aware of the commercial circumstances of [the organisation] and that they judge related issues accordingly.

Key messages

1. The organisation is financially viable, stable and has begun the process of planning and working to survive and emerge from the current position.

2. Staff throughout the organisation's locations will be an essential element of this recovery process.

3. The organisation values the efforts and contribution made by staff in various locations and is acting on the intelligence gathered in recent months in order to help strengthen the business plan in order to be able to offer higher levels of job security.

Target audiences

1. Employees in the US, Europe and South East Asia.

2. Their families and influencers.

3. The various staff associations and unions to which some employees belong.

Strategy

The new business plan will be communicated in person by [the Vice President] to all staff in a series of face to face presentations during the two weeks beginning 7 April 1997. He will give information on the current business, financial, sales and product development programmes and will take questions from the floor. He will also issue a leave-behind document summarising this presentation.

Further information on progress, together with the opportunity for them to gain further information, to reply to points and to make their own suggestions, will then be provided for all employees on e-mail during the next five months. In October, [the VP] will again visit all locations to provide an update on progress.

Methodology

[The VP] will make presentations at staff meetings in the following locations on the following dates [a list then followed]. The leave behind document will be devised centrally with the input of appropriate staff from each location and will then be territorialised for each location.

Responsibility for co-ordinating location presentations will lie with [the team was named.]

Responsibility for frequent e-mail progress reports following the first wave of presentations will be assumed by [and a further team was named].

There followed a few more details, such as costs and logistics and that was that. The plan was widely accepted, put into place and worked very well. The organisation is now looking at a renewed assault on key markets, which are gradually bringing about an increase in market share, sales volumes and profitability. The worst of the hump seems to be over, although the recession in manufacturing industry in various parts of the world, including the UK, has made the recovery slower than was hoped. Nevertheless, in essence this was, and is, a very basic internal communications plan which worked.

The task of putting the plan into operation is relatively easy, although there may need to be some careful consideration given to the logistics of the exercise. Taking the example above, the American management had to work out very carefully exactly where and when they were going to appear on their road show. The danger is that, given the jungle telegraph which is always quicker than any carefully constructed plan can be, the news reaches venues before the person who is supposed to be giving it.

Often, the best way of dealing with this is to put employees on their honour not to reveal all the details of the presentation to their colleagues in advance of another presentation. In any case, the fine details of the impact of change upon locations is usually subtly different.

Another way is to organise simultaneous presentations – or as near as can be achieved – and this works equally well provided there are enough good senior presenters to cover all the locations at more or less the same time.

In many organisations, this is a problem. No matter how senior the manager, the fear of presenting in public is a real one. Even an absolute monarch like Louis XIV lived in dread of it ("Like every reflective person I . . . suffered from timidity, especially when I had to speak at length in public"), while a well-known survey in the US a few years ago showed that public speaking ranked second after only death in the list of businessmen's phobias.

Here, then, is an important point to bear in mind when planning. There must be a sufficient number of high quality, experienced presenters in the senior management ranks if the presentations are to succeed. A bad presentation to employees is worse than no presentation at all because it shows the audience the faults of the management in whom they are supposed to be putting their trust. Building confidence on the back of an inept public display is a doubly difficult exercise and one which no self-respecting internal communications function wants to have to face.

Two-way Communications

Another aspect to plan into the whole exercise and continuing process is the right of reply. One-way communication is not true communication and will not be tolerated for long by many employees. So, whether it be a session in the presentation set aside for questions (in which case, both they and the answers need to be very carefully rehearsed in advance) or whether it's an e-mail or postal address through which employees can set out their reactions and thoughts, it needs to be planned if it is to work properly – and if it doesn't work properly, there will be plenty of complaints.

Sometimes, management will resent this right of reply, mainly on the grounds of insecurity. This is anathema to an organisation that truly wants to improve its communications and is one of the first points of principle, which any internal communications incumbent should try to get across to senior managers. It isn't always easy, because attitudes become entrenched, but it's a lot easier than trying to break a strike.

Another point to remember in planning is that, although the impact may be made during a single campaign or exercise, the process of communicating internally carries on all the time. It isn't just a one-off road show or series of cascade briefings but a continuous process designed to impart necessary or desirable information at all times. This overall communications approach, not just focused sessions or vehicles, but full-time communications, is key to success. Short blasts of effort are all very well and sometimes work effectively, but they cannot replace the continuing effort. Instead they must co-exist with that effort and help to create the climate of confidence that is vital to any successful communications culture.

Finally there are the choices between verbal and written communications, and direct and indirect approaches.

Methods

Much management time is spent on getting written communications for employees down to a fine art – and it is clearly a very important aspect of communicating. There is, however, a difficulty with it. In many countries, literacy levels are not very high; a UN report in September 1998 showed that, for all practical purposes, over 20 per cent of British adults are illiterate. Further, it was reported in June 1998 that in some British secondary schools, up to 40 per cent of 16 year olds left school without even one GCSE – the national exam system which includes English as a basic subject. "Many 16 year olds were barely literate or numerate" the report concluded.

Some, but not all, of these teenagers become employees. If they are unable, or unwilling, to read, the effectiveness of an in-house newsletter is severely restricted. Moreover, many people in many countries, although nominally literate, dislike reading. Computers, television and video screens have bred a distaste for, and impatience with, the written word, a fact which betokens ill for the future. Teenagers in particular, now relatively computer literate, are rather less literate, in the traditional sense of the word, than their parents.

There is also the question of employees who are working in a language, which is not their mother tongue. Vauxhall Motors, for example, has around 20 per cent of its workforce in the UK whose native language is not English (it is mainly Gujerati). While it is courteous to translate all material, it does slow down the process of disseminating information and creates possibilities for confusion and mistranslation; it is another link in the chain of possible human error.

Some societies have come to terms with these global issues. Health education programmes in the Middle East, for example, tend to be carried out largely by video. In Saudi Arabia in the early-1980s it was quite common for Bedu women to give birth squatting in the sand in a goatskin tent while watching colour videos of *Dallas*! The way to get over messages about health in the Middle East, therefore, is to show people on screen doing the things you want the audience to do – washing, feeding, taking simple health precautions and so on. No amount of words can convey the same immediacy of message as the magic box in the corner of the room – or tent.

As in all things, a balance is desirable. As a general rule, for the purposes of planning, no verbal presentation should be left without a written document that contains the main messages. If it is omitted, the presentation can be open to interpretation – and that is something that most employers want to minimise. Equally, very few internal communications programmes can exist by the written word alone – even when e-mail and intranets, are taken into account. There needs to be a human face, a personality to the message-conveying process, and this can only be provided by humans.

Direct or indirect is the other major question at this stage. Do you talk directly to the employees or do you involve external channels to help reinforce the message? This is a very complex issue and one that will be dealt with in a later chapter. Suffice it to say for now that, if an internal communications function is harnessing external forces, it must be done very subtly and very cleverly, otherwise it could all blow up in the face of the instigator. Not many organisations are that clever.

CHAPTER SEVEN

The Wind from the East

Globalism

Employees are, to any professional communicator, the hardest possible audience with whom they will ever have to communicate. As we have seen in previous chapters, they already know so much about the organisation and its successes and failures that they cannot be fobbed off with some of the glib patter which can sometimes satisfy external audiences.

They also have an expectation to be told the whole truth – and sometimes, considerably more than that. That is a not unreasonable expectation, especially if the organisation is undergoing change, as many are at any given time. What is less easy to fathom, in the eyes of some managers, is the attitude that drives this expectation. How much does the average employee, if there is such a thing, really know about the organisation which pays his/her wages? What are the employees' preconceptions? What are their prejudices, for they undeniably exist in some minds?

Without knowing the answers to these and similar questions, it is very difficult to plan the communications properly, as we saw in the previous chapter. This is why the research element of the planning process is so critical to the success of the overall effort.

When planning the research process, it is also worthwhile remembering some of the more influential factors that help to determine logistics. Where, for instance, do the majority of the employees work? If they are all concentrated in one head office with relatively easy interflow of communication, then the nature of the communications campaign or longer programme will be dictated by this factor. If, on the other hand, they are spread through the country, or even across a continent, the methods of communicating are going to have to be more sophisticated in order to cope with the greater complexity of message distribution and differing timescales, cultures and languages. It is this element of globalism, which is becoming ever more important as internal communications practitioners are faced with the task of organising and managing communications to different nations, cultures, creeds and attitudes. Logistics apart, and they can be hard enough, this can be a daunting prospect.

Examples of attitudes and values from elsewhere in the world, therefore, can help to form a more accurate idea of the key question of attitude; what is desirable and what is acceptable in social terms or in employment systems wherever you work? Increasingly, for example, the values and attitudes of the Far East and South East Asia are being subjected to closer scrutiny in the

West, partly because many Western organisations are now active in those ASEAN and Chinese markets. This is partly because Asia is becoming the centre of economic and mercantile power in the world and partly because some Western methods, attitudes and values are simply not working, or are being exposed as outmoded, narrow in scope and execution, counter productive and uncompetitive.

So, what form does internal communications take in the tiger economy nations and how can it provide food for thought in Western commercial society? How does it relate to Western industrial democracy and how far is it a set of values which is unlikely to find favour with the average European or American employee? Are there are lessons from the Orient which we can learn in countries such as the UK, or does the Asian set of values though excellent in its own domain, not translate to other countries?

Language

To start with, to communicate in the natural business language of the organisation is not only good sense, it is also common courtesy. There is a mini-debate going on at the time of writing about the element of ethnicity in internal communications, which was touched on in Chapter 6. Polyglot societies can throw fresh light on this issue. In Singapore, for example, virtually all the communication is carried out in English as the business language of the world with which Singapore has dealings. This is becoming less rigid a rule as the Anglo-American-Australian influence begins to wane in the face of massive demand from China, where English is still not as widespread as throughout the rest of developed Asia. Even the Japanese multinationals operating out of Singapore expect to carry out their work in English and some employ native English speaking, non-Singaporeans, usually British or Americans, to represent them in this way.

Over the border in Malaysia, however, life is less straightforward – and may well reflect some of the situations to be found in many large and complex organisations in other parts of the world. For a start, the official language is Bahasa Melayu, which must be used in all dealings with the government. Yet English is still the business language that most educated Malaysians will use in their work. So there is a need to issue many documents and statements in two languages. This appears to be somewhat unnecessary to the outsider, although less so than the situation in Belgium where French and Walloon sit uneasily side by side and require a total duplication of linguistic bureaucracy.

Culture

So it is with many organisations. The form in which the employees wish to be addressed, not just in a particular language but in a particular style or format indicative of a set of values and attitudes, is an important piece of knowledge without which no internal communicator should be acting. We are not just talking about language but about cultures, rights, attitudes and expectations. Taking the Malaysian example a step further, there is a gently stated, but politely enforced, code of conduct when dealing with Malays which embodies certain standards of protocol and decorum. The traditions and values of Malaysia differ significantly from those of the West. For instance, Malaysians perceive 'Man' (as in mankind or human kind) as being separate from nature in Western traditions. Western man is seen as a master who harnesses and exploits nature for his purposes. In the Eastern tradition, Man is viewed as part of nature and has to integrate with, and adapt to, the environment. He is subservient to, or in harmony with, nature.

Consequently, the approach to many apparently clear-cut issues tends to be less than clear-cut when viewed in the light of these different perceptions. Environmental policies, for example, take on a much more meaningful role in the context of these differences, as do attitudes to career development, sales, ambition, power, management and communications.

Again, the Malaysians view human relationships differently. They believe that the Western tradition emphasises the individual; a person sets his or her own goals and tries to achieve them through his/her own efforts, solving his/her own problems. In Malaysia, a person is regarded as a member of a family, a collective whose behaviour is aimed at building smooth interpersonal relationships. Dependence on others is encouraged because it strengthens relationships among people; so communal feelings supersede the incentive to excel over others. Relationships are hierarchical, as they used to be in the West, and people are treated according to their position in society. Consequently, any differences are often handled through an intermediary in order to avoid losing face.

Perhaps an application of this type of philosophy might help some Western organisations to realise the value of their employees a little more fully. Moreover, many organisations now deal extensively with South East Asia and, if they don't at the moment, they probably will in a few years' time, so the points may be valuable to many Western internal communicators.

Values

Take, for instance, the assumptions of values on which Malaysians work. The Malaysian Institute of Management (MIM) has developed a series of tables of ethnic values which make interesting reading. It lists, as values for Malays, the following:

- respect for elders;
- spirituality;
- humility;

- face;
- tact;
- generosity;
- caring;
- patience;
- feelings;
- hospitality;
- honesty;
- rituals;
- budi – a tacit system of reciprocal obligations;
- friendliness;
- politeness;
- harmony/peace;
- loyalty;
- apologetic;
- formalities;
- accommodating;
- trustworthiness;
- discipline;
- teamwork;
- sense of appropriateness;
- indirect;
- ceremonial;
- non-aggressive;
- co-operative;
- well mannered;
- devout;
- family oriented;
- obedience;
- fairness;
- sincerity;
- courtesy;
- self-respect;
- non-confrontational;
- tolerance;
- compliance.

This long list makes fascinating reading because it probably embodies most of the qualities which Western managers would very much appreciate in their employees. Perhaps it embodies the type of employee they would like – one who is obedient, hard-working and non-confrontational. Perhaps it is the ideal towards which to work, not in the sense of removing individuality, there is plenty of that in Malaysia, but of replacing some of the regard for self with a little more regard for the entity for which the employee works.

Now compare these values with the list the same authority has drawn up for Westerners, mainly, it believes, for Americans:

- individualism;
- success;
- punctuality;
- equality;
- assertiveness – not to be confused with aggression;
- achievement;
- hard work;
- privacy;
- competition;
- directness;
- independence;
- freedom of speech;
- informality;
- innovation;
- frankness;
- openness;

Which group of values is easier to manage?

Take, for, instance, the influence of some of these ethnic values in the workplace as identified by MIM.

> Generally, subordinates will not argue with their boss for it will be seen as a loss of face to the boss.

When was the last time you remember that happening in your office? Yet, wouldn't it be a more harmonious organisation if people subscribed to that view and carried it out in practice? In some large organisations for which I have worked, at least 75 per cent of manager time, effort and energy went into internal politicking rather than getting on with the business of developing and manufacturing product or service, selling it and making profits or satisfying customers.

Had even a fraction of that effort gone into improving the ways in which we carried out our business, a number of British companies would be in a better shape than they currently are – and a lot more jobs would have been preserved in the UK with consequent beneficial effects upon prosperity and social justice.

Nor should we imagine that the Malaysian approach is one that would only be adopted in the West by a self-effacing sheep. Malaysians can be very assertive and very persuasive and, while their society is by no means perfect, it isn't doing badly by any standards. The future of world economic influence certainly does not lie in Threadneedle Street, Wall Street, Paris or Frankfurt any more. Despite the recent economic hiccup, no global player with any pretensions to covering the world markets is going to be able to afford not to be in South East Asia and the Far East within a very few years.

Moreover, the influence of values like this in an organisational culture can be very far-reaching. There is, for instance, the underlying value of respect for seniors, of preserving face and avoiding embarrassment for others. This might sound like pie in the sky but in Malaysia, and elsewhere in the East, it actually works.

Asian Management

In Malaysia, too, an authoritative style of management is still predominant and usually well tolerated. Subordinates are expected to be loyal to their employers in a way that reflects parental loyalty and family relationships. When it is analysed, this is the same kind of approach that the more enlightened Western employers are trying to foster – Anita Roddick at The Body Shop, for example, or Mars with their insistence that employees are actually business associates. There is the atmosphere not so much of 'us and them' or of employers and employees but of a series of partners in a venture, of associates in a company that is directly comparable to the Asian feeling of oneness with its underlying value of loyalty within a healthy respect for authority.

Yet the ability to disagree is still present. Singapore is the most demanding country in the world for management trainers. It is not uncommon for a delegate to say, at 4.55pm, "But, Mr Greener, you have just said X and this morning, at 9.10am, you said Y. Please, how do these two statements correlate?" Very polite, very incisive, very firm and quite unexpected – the first time you go. If there is disagreement, they will cloak it in courtesy, but they will also persist in making their point until they get what appears to be a solution to the dichotomy they perceive. Let nobody in the West be naive enough to believe that Asians are too polite to argue. They simply do not need to resort to public or semi-public arguments with all the connotations of unseemly fuss, loss of dignity and lasting divisiveness. Further:

> Malaysians work extremely well in a team environment, partly because it is fuelled by their sense of belonging. The spirit of collectivism is more important than individualism and this is often translated into the willingness to give priority to group interest ahead of individual concerns. Satisfaction at work comes from having opportunities to receive respect from colleagues and creating harmonious, predicable and enjoyable friendships with both subordinates and peers.

If only we could inculcate that kind of collectivism into some Western institutions, without stifling the innovation and creativity which already exist, albeit in dormant fashion in many cases. Yet, is it really so hard to move towards this type of culture and set of values? Aren't they already present, if only we could harness them more tightly and focus them more sharply?

> Malaysians also dislike overt displays of anger or other aggressive behaviour. An aggressive, go-getting, abrasive manager may be perceived as brash, rough and insensitive to the feelings of others as well as discourteous and embarrassing. He/she may also threaten social harmony and cause his staff to become withdrawn and non-contributory.

Isn't this what we have done too much in states like the UK and the US? Innovation, dynamic leadership, managing by brute force and ignorance are all very well, occasionally necessary and often easier than any collective style, but, if they worked all that well, why is it that the UK balance of payments keeps getting wider, that unemployment will probably now remain at relatively high levels, that export order books are flagging and that economic influence is steadily seeping away? Of course, there are many other factors (exchange rates, the emergence of new industrialised nations with a wealth of raw materials and cheap labour, domestic complacency, a fixation with affording an unaffordable welfare state and a reluctance to get hands dirty too many times) but surely employee attitudes is also a factor in this process.

> There is a tendency to deal with ambiguities and uncertainties by using the indirect approach of a third party. Bad news becomes more palatable to the recipient when communicated through a respectable party.

That is a very interesting point of view and one that has a substantial bearing on the way in which some internal communications are carried out. We will look later at the role of indirect communications in the whole internal communications framework and we will see the sense of sometimes not going about the task in direct, blatant and possibly provocative fashion.

The use of an intermediary to make first contact with a prospective client is important for establishing goodwill and trust. In this
way the prospective client can raise issues which otherwise would
be difficult to do in the presence of the person seeking the business.

How often do we do this in practice without necessarily formalising it in this
way? We prefer to have suppliers recommended by third parties whose opinions we trust, we often canvas third party opinion in relatively normal acts of
business – buying a product or service, for example. By extending the principles a little further into the workplace, maybe we can achieve a greater level
of satisfaction with our suppliers and other business partners – and even our
own employees? This, again, could avoid unseemly and unproductive squabbling.

So, there are some collective values which work pretty well in Malaysia
in terms of internal communications; could they work equally well in the
West? For example, the focus on collectivity, which can emerge as a need to
be part of a group, to serve as an emotional safety valve, especially for employees who are not comfortable in communicating their frustrations about
their job directly to their superiors. Importantly, it also helps newcomers to
assimilate themselves into the workplace very smoothly and easily – another
bonus from which, perhaps, we in the West could benefit.

The relationship orientation tends to see relationships based on an un-
written code covering relations with peers, superiors and subordinates and
equate them to family style relationships in order to make them easier to
define and, thus to cope with.

Respect

The respect for elders is also a telling point as a value in internal communications. A manager in London once stated that "you have to earn respect",
quite right, yet, in Asian circles, leaders are often considered as wise elders
and their authority is often unquestioned in the sense that they are not seriously challenged as they are in the West. Often subordinates will show their
respect by allowing the most senior and experienced staff to speak first in a
meeting and set the tone for the proceedings. This is exactly what we do in
many formal types of meeting – boards, councils, committees, political groups,
and so on. Yet, if we were to carry this innate respect through to more
workplaces, wouldn't they be pleasanter and more fruitful places in which to
work together successfully? And wouldn't this, therefore, go part of the way
towards achieving an inherent objective of successful internal communications?

Loyalty is another concept closely related to respect. Malaysian managers have a moral obligation to care for their employees in return for loyalty

and commitment – almost like an extended family. As loyalty is highly valued, employers expect their employees to be dedicated to their work and loyal to their organisations.

One of the training games which hardly ever fails to provoke different thinking about delegates' organisations is to ask them to draw a picture of what their organisation means to them. The results vary greatly from Picasso's cubist period to a plethora of logos, globes, computers, buildings and Lowry-like people. Very occasionally, delegates are tempted to write simply a large £ or $. This is a very sad reflection on their relationship with their organisations. Given that they are going to spend around 75 per cent of their waking lives at work, assuming that they work from leaving school or college to normal retirement age, isn't it a pity that all that work means to them is the ability to pay the mortgage, go out and get drunk or escape on holidays to far away places? That situation has never happened in all the years I've been training in Asia – but it has happened several times in the UK.

The hierarchy of an organisation is another Asian trait closely related to loyalty and respect. The polite system requires one to know the correct way of salutation as this indicates good manners and a realistic perception of the organisational structure – doing it right may enhance the social and professional standing of the employee and enhance his/her confidence at the same time, doing it wrong may have the opposite effect.

This is not a perpetuation of an outmoded class struggle so beloved of Marxist/Leninist scribblers, but a pragmatic and honest reflection of the way reality sits in the structure of the organisation. It is as absurd to pretend that all societies are egalitarian as it is to pretend that all employees are born with the same skills and ambition to develop those skills. The very recognition of that fact is sometimes overlooked, even by internal communicators.

Harmony

Malaysians also feel happy in their work if they enjoy harmonious relationships with their colleagues, and they are then more secure in their role, in their employment and in their ambition to do what is best for their employer because that will ultimately benefit all who work for the organisation. It is a practical kind of communism, a throwback to the commune system which is still, perhaps, the most likely form of communism to work in practice – when the ingredients are present. But, as George Orwell pointed out, some animals are more equal than others and it would be unwise to take this ideal too far in the millennium-haunted West.

Finally, Malaysians respect what they call 'jaga maruah' (or 'lien mentzu' in Chinese). We would call it saving face, but it means more than that. It has connotations of dignity in and at work, of self-standing in the eyes on one's colleagues which are not adequately expressed in the bare translation of 'saving face'.

Self-respect

One of the most important aspects of working, surely, is to preserve dignity in oneself, to preserve self-respect and self-esteem. The employee who sees his/her job as a £ or a $ sign is unlikely to have much of that dignity or self-respect. Most of the managers you will ever meet are preoccupied, even haunted, by a fear of what other people may think of them – of saving face, in extreme terms. Yet, with the right approach to harmonious working relationships and open, honest internal communications, much of this fear can be removed because it is often based on ignorance of what others know and suspicion of what others might think, without knowing the true facts. Isn't openness of communication worth a good deal of effort to get rid of this Damoclean sword of low self-worth?

There is clearly a need in any organisation for managers to build a strong and productive workforce with values that are consistent with the cultural ethos of that organisation. With the advent of globalism, technological advancement and the need for a skilled but affordable workforce, some values must be continuously reassessed for their relevance and applicability. For example, managers may have to discourage work practices that are not in harmony and could be counter-productive to productivity. Equally, they need to identify new work values that can be developed into shared practice.

In promoting new values and practice, however, care needs to be taken that there is no apparent or inherent conflict between what management wants to do and what the workforce wants to preserve – especially status and entitlements. We can remember the dreaded days of eroding differentials which eventually made the British worker the laughing stock of the developed world. Strikes over the length of a tea break or the time it takes an engine driver to walk the length of a train seem to embody the intransigence and apparent pettiness of the values dear to the workforce, the preservation of which caused strident unions to take extreme action.

The ideal blend would seem to be to try to preserve the richness of a proud heritage while adopting new work values, such as some of those outlined above, values which can promote flexibility and productivity in the workplace. In this context, being able to use behaviours appropriate to the inter-cultural, intra-cultural and cross-cultural levels will enable the organisation to evolve a work culture where there is harmony, synergy and understanding within an increasingly multi-cultural workforce.

In the context of this book, the main difference between South East Asian and Western managers is the manner in which these goals are pursued. The conventional wisdom is that in the West, the task is primary while the harmonious relationship may become secondary. In South East Asia, most managers believe that the task should certainly be achieved, but not at the cost of non-harmonious relationships because that will sap the ability of the organisation to work effectively.

Accordingly, to follow the Asian approach, managers need to allocate time and energy to build relationships through consistent internal communications based on trust and understanding.

The Malaysian Institute of Management has again summed it up very neatly; both sets of managers have the common goal of task achievement. The Eastern paradigm is one based on harmonious relationships, collectivism and shame culture; the Western paradigm is perceived as being based on self-actualisation, individualism and the guilt culture. Maybe, the utopia lies somewhere between the two, but perhaps, like the original Garden of Eden, it lies nearer the East than the West.

CHAPTER EIGHT

The Direct Approach to Communication

The Written Route: Creating the Message

In most cases, the direct approach is better than the indirect approach, which we shall look at later. Directness in communications is usually a virtue, even though the messages to be communicated do not always lend themselves to the most direct type of expression.

For a start, directness betokens honesty; few people are likely to hold a grudge if they see that the manager is trying his/her hardest to be open and sincere through direct communications. Many misunderstandings can be cleared up by being direct; it may not make the communicator popular and there is certainly such a fault as being too direct, but this doesn't often arise in internal communications.

Secondly, even if the news is bad, employees usually want to hear it straight from the horse's mouth. Pussyfooting about through all sorts of different media and experimenting with different channels to tell employees something is not often appreciated by the employees themselves. Here, once again, the role of the line manager is crucial. If he or she normally communicates with the employees in that section but is replaced by somebody else for a particularly sensitive announcement, the damage done to the trust and confidence in which that manager is held by his/her employees can be very substantial. He/she is seen as being good enough for the day to day drudgery but not senior enough or responsible enough to be entrusted to communicate anything really important. Maybe, that manager doesn't even know the content of the communication – and this is not a case of ignorance being bliss.

Of course there are, as we have seen, many instances when the line manager cannot be expected to carry out all the communication, times when the organisation needs to do it on a scatter shot approach to all its employees at more or less the same time. For this purpose, there are three major options: the written route, the verbal approach and the electronic route, such as e-mail.

We will address the second two of these approaches in the next few chapters. In this chapter we shall look at the traditional route of communicating by the written word, try to see how best to create those words and look at some examples of best, and not so best, practice.

There is, of course, an ideal fusion of all three routes and this we will also address later. For a moment, we will focus purely on the most common, most basic and most traditional method of communicating to employees: the internal document.

Research

This can take many forms, bulletins, briefings, minutes, magazines, newspapers and newsletters, employee annual reports and a host of other pieces of paper. Some work better than others in some organisations; in other organisations, they are mostly on the way out.

One thing they nearly all have in common – they have to be written. This may sound self-evident, but it is undeniably the case and it is often the stage at which written communications falls flat on its face. We have already looked at who should create this written document. Now it is time to look at how it should be created. Starting the process of creating the message brings us back to our old friend planning and its first base camp, research.

It is usually a good idea to research your audience so that you can think the same way in which the audience thinks. All internal communications staff should know broadly the conditions in which employees work, should have experienced these conditions for themselves and should know, roughly, what is involved in the work. The worst accusation that can be levelled at many internal communications practitioners is that they do not know the type of working conditions in which their audiences operate.

Identifying with the Audience

Often it is a good idea to spend time with different sections of employees to experience at first hand the pressures, attitudes, routines and opinions that prevail. Anyone who has ever worked in a warehouse, for example, will never look at the business in the same way again. 'Goods-in' takes on a new meaning, the complexities of storage and distribution become unravelled. Pallets are no longer confused in size and strange new terms, such as 'stilich', come into the course of everyday language. 'Trolleys' and 'wheels' assume new meanings, 'picking' becomes a term associated with collecting a variety of goods for a customer order and all kinds of colloquialisms never before encountered appear in the consciousness.

What this amounts to is almost a working language in its own right. Indeed, if the example were of an office in a high tech industry, it probably would be a totally new language. While this sort of terminology is common parlance to those who use it, the patois involved can almost create a clique of employees, an elite who understand what they mean and, in its most extreme form, revel in the fact that outsiders do not.

There is a tradition which may or may not be apocryphal, about an engineering factory in which apprentices used to go through a process of being told by their supervisor to go to the foreman of the paint shop, which was at the very far side of the site about half a mile away, and ask the foreman of the paint shop if they could borrow the long weight, "not the short one but the long one, mind". The wretched youth would go, find the foreman with difficulty and pose the question. The standard reply was always to "hang on there" while the paint shop foreman went away, presumably to find the long weight.

About an hour later he would return, empty handed and say, "Right, son, you've had your long wait, you'd better get back now." Hardly the quintessence of wit, but a tradition about which it is better to be forewarned than to be kept in ignorance. Equally, if even an oblique reference can be made to it in a company publication, the respect of those concerned is immediately kindled, because they recognise that somebody knows what goes on on the shop floor and the complaint for too long has been that management are not in touch with the shop floor, do not care and are unlikely to start to do so.

By using the language, traditions and humour of the workforce, the internal communications practitioner begins to put himself/herself on the same plane, begins to think like their audience, begins to identify with them and to be acknowledged by them as someone who knows what is what in the real world of work, not just in the perceived, pampered environment of an office.

Communicators from the organisation, whatever it may be, will always find it harder to break down any resistance to organisational messages unless they know about this language and can refer to it, without necessarily using it, so that their audience at least begins to respect them for knowing something about the way in which they operate.

All offices, industries, businesses, public sector organisations and most other groups have their own professional patois. Most guard it jealously, many continue to develop it to keep pace with modern developments. One BBC television commentator was heard to say recently that a cricket umpire had 'negatived' an appeal. Does this clumsy use of English really help a modern audience to understand what he means? Isn't there an easier to understand and less ambiguous alternative, such as 'turned down'?

The IT industry alone has given us a number of particularly ugly uses of language over the last couple of decades: 'dustbin' used as a verb, violent sounding phrases such as 'booting up' and 'crashing', most of which have found their way into a wider usage. It was probably the same 150 years ago, when navvies were building railways and canals, or early in the 20th century when engineering factories were starting up, but their traditions have partly been lost. The secrets of their patois are now remembered only by a few survivors. The same will no doubt happen to IT language in a few years' time. Who now, for instance, remembers the 'viffing' of Harrier jump jets during the Falklands war of 1982?

As part of the process of acquiring this atmosphere and inside knowledge, shadowing is strongly recommended for all internal communications staff as part of their induction process or, at least, as part of their developmental process. Not all areas may need to be shadowed, but the more representative ones do. This helps to protect internal communications practitioners from the worst accusation made against them: that they do not understand the circumstances in which other employees, their audiences, work. This is especially important with employees who do not work from head office, or from any office, such as field engineers or remote outposts of an organisation.

After shadowing, it is easier to relate the findings of research and experience with employees to the way in which the communication is created. It is also worth remembering a few of the more common rules of successful communication with any audience. For example, on the basis that the average adult reading age in the UK is just 13 years old, keep words simple and sentences short.

At first, this may seem unnecessary. But, think back to what you were reading when you were thirteen: Biggles, Arthur Ransome, Alan Garner, Henry Treece, maybe top-end Enid Blyton or the beginnings of PG Wodehouse. That is the level at which the vast majority of British people (and, therefore, most employees) cease to develop their reading skills. It follows that anything much more complicated is going to elude or bore them.

While this may not be a particularly scintillating reflection on the standard of British education, it is reality and, at best, we are stuck with it for the foreseeable future in internal communication terms. Major advances in education, if attainable at all, are unlikely to affect this situation for at least a decade and, even then, only marginally. Indeed, there is a suggestion that the situation is worsening all the time; eight years ago, the average reading age was 13 years and 8 months; now it's 13 years and 2 months.

There are exceptions, of course. A management consultancy, stockbroker or merchant bank, for example, would expect its staff to have a generally higher level of literacy. Unfortunately, the same cannot be said for many organisations where the rule for internal communications has to be to reduce language to the lowest common denominator. This does not mean talking down to people or patronising them in any way. Talking in simple language is far less patronising than giving employees great wads of pompously written information and expecting them to understand it. That amounts to an insult.

Simplicity

So, be very direct and very honest. Introduce only one idea at a time so that it has time to enter the consciousness, penetrate to a satisfactory level and, hopefully, be understood. It is far better to get across one idea properly than to try to communicate three at once and fail to get any of them clearly understood.

Keep the language simple, so that employees don't have to reach for a dictionary every few words. They are unlikely to make the effort or to show themselves up in public by doing this, anyway, so all confusing language achieves is alienation and a sense of injustice that the employee is being put into this position in the first place. Grudges based on an apparent slight to the intelligence of the employee, whether based in fact or not, are very difficult to overcome and take a great deal of very clear and honest communication and a massive amount of skill on the part of the offending manager. Very rarely is this combination forthcoming.

Avoid jargon that is not going to be understood by the vast majority of employees. It is one thing to show that you know how they think and talk; it is quite another to expect them to understand TLAs and lots of in-jargon and terminology which may be more the preserve of the board room, sales team or IT department – especially the latter. Some internal documents use a high degree of jargon as matter of course and this may be accepted as part and parcel of the overall method of working. Take the following case of a motor industry plant newsletter.

> In Car Final, the Standardised Inspection Process (SIP) is being upgraded to incorporate a quality call flagging poor quality. Eight of thirteen inspection stations now have the alarm in place. Attention is focused on quality defects shown up during Internal Audit (IUVA) Compound Audit (GDS) and customer complaints (warranty).
>
> Once such a defect is discovered an escalation procedure is put into place. The inspector presses the quality alarm button playing a quality tune specific to that inspection station. This alerts local supervision and, if this fails to generate a response, successively more senior Quality Assurance and production management are called by telephone. Finally, if Unit Managers have been unable to attend the inspector will stop the track – closing the quality gate.

To most of us lay people, this is pretty well approaching garbage, but to people involved in production and quality control at whom it is aimed, it appears to do the trick of telling them what they need to know without too much problem. The English is tortuous and slightly pompous but it conveys what the authors want it to say – the new quality procedure. Quite how the abbreviations manage to represent phrases the words of which start with totally different letters is a mystery that is probably best left to those in the production plant. Suffice it to say that, as far as the company in which this happens in concerned, it does the job it needs to do.

Or, take this from the same source.

> Target Build for May was 65.5 per cent bringing the YTD aver-

age to 63 per cent against a Target of 86 per cent for Yr98. Pilot build at Plant A of two pre-production vehicles is now complete. Pre-prod. will be carried out in three phases; in Phase 1, 25 vehicles will be built mid-June. Phases 2 and 3 are solely for vehicles which the new Diesel engine 19 will be built in Phase 2 early in July and a further 38 in Phase 3 immediately after the closure, coincident with POS for the remainder of our new vehicle build. POS for the X1 variant is planned for 22 September. The new engine is a high pressure variant of the current direct injection diesel delivering PS compared to the PS of the low blow unit.

Although one or two terms have been changed to preserve anonymity, it was probably unnecessary. Very few people outside an automotive engineering plant would make head or tail of this kind of message. Yet it is time-honoured speak inside such a plant and it seems to work – once employees have become accustomed to the stilted language. However, like most systems, it gradually takes over the employees and then they can barely remember a time when they didn't use it. What's worse, they often can't understand why newcomers can't understand it. By contrast the very next line shows much more simply, the main news that employees want to read:

> Productivity Bonus Payments for May totalled £145.90 a weekly average of £36.48.

That's one message that nobody will misunderstand.

Idiosyncratic or not, the struggle to change this sort of thing is probably an unequal one, given that this type of communications is usually left to engineers who are not going to take kindly to anyone telling them how to talk to each other. As the old civil engineers' phrase goes: "When I was a student, I could never spell the word 'engineer'. Now I are one."

Three letter abbreviations (TLAs) can be particularly annoying and confusing. Take this extract from a government White Paper, admittedly often a rich source of confusion and annoyance for most citizens:

> It could also bid to contract out work to RTBs and other bodies; separate funding would also be provided by DCMS for RDAs and the GLA to work with RTBs and other bodies to support tourism in the regions ... "

Although not directly aimed at employees, this discussion paper is so dense in jargon as to be pretty well unintelligible to anyone else; could that be deliberate as a way of preserving a mystique which, in itself, is an accepted way of preserving jobs, especially in the public sector? It's an old trick but it might still work.

Still in the public sector, below is a letter from the chief executive officer of a local authority to employees and other stakeholders.

> I am writing to inform you of the Council's position on the Local Government Review . . . The Council expressed great disappointment at the decision, as concerns remain about the implications for costs, disruption to services, and the lack of public support for change . . . The Council's other major concern is that because, at the outset of the review, no one expected the hybrid solution (where a unitary authority is created alongside a continuing, smaller Council) to prove to be the most common solution, across the country (which, of course, has proven to be the case), little thought has been given by the Department of Environment and others to the full implications of such a solution. Such thought as has been given has concentrated on the implications of such a solution for those covered by the new unitary authority. Hardly any consideration at all has been given to the implications for those living in the smaller continuing Council area.

There is much more of this in a closely printed two-page letter aimed at a wider audience than purely employees and it is all in the same tone. There are many things wrong with it as a piece of communication, no matter how sincere the feeling behind it. A few points will suffice.

First the tone is whining, betraying a constant complaint which may or may not be justified. The writer however, does not add to the justice of his or her cause by couching it all in such a negative and whinging tone. The structure of the sentences is convoluted and ties up both the writer and the readers in knots (the rest of the letter digs an even deeper grave for itself in this respect).

The use of contradictions is unfortunate, to say the least. How, for instance, can "hardly any consideration at all" be a logical statement? Either some consideration has been given, or none at all has been given. Writers cannot have it both ways. The use of parentheses doesn't help to clarify the position, either; by the time the reader has got through yet another set of brackets, it is difficult to remember what the original sentence was all about.

The basics of grammar are interesting, "which has proven to be the case" is not one of the most effortless phrases in the English language and would sit very uncomfortably in normal speech. If the rest of the letter could be quoted the amount of repetition would be seen to be awesome. Above all, the unrelenting negativity of tone is the biggest killer in a letter, which was, presumably, intended to rally the troops both inside and outside the authority in the face of perceived adversity.

There needs to be some positive aspect to all communications. To give gloom and doom and expect people, especially employees, to respond positively to new challenges is self-defeating and betokens a lack of self-confidence which is worrying in any letter from a chief executive figure. Employees want to be reassured that their bosses, especially their leader, has his or her finger on the pulse and is equal to any reasonable threat posed to the organisation. This letter does not convey any such confidence; all it does is complain that the toys are being taken away. Such barely concealed petulance hardly becomes a chief executive in private, let alone in public. When it is communicated so blatantly to the employees whose future may hang on the ability of that chief executive to cope with imposed change, the inevitable conclusion is that the chief executive has probably been over promoted and is incapable of carrying out his/her role professionally.

Journalism Models

Journalism is a valuable source of writing lore, partly because this is where such lore has been successfully developed over several generations in a highly competitive sector. Without necessarily resorting to pure journalese, there are a number of rules observed by journalists that can often greatly benefit internal communications practitioners.

So, for example, in writing to employees and other stakeholders, take *The Sun* newspaper as a model writing style for mass communications. *The Times* is an equally good example for managerial communications. Neither style has to be acquiescent but both have to be responsible in their own way.

Before anyone starts to pour scorn on *The Sun*, let us remember that *The Sun*, *The Star* and *The Mirror* between them are read by nearly half (46 per cent) the population of the UK every single day. As manipulators of a mass market, they are unrivalled in newsprint and exceeded only by the power of television. That is due both to clever and successful writing, as well as layout, editorial policy and marketing. They are not just about scantily clad young women; indeed, increasingly they are not about that aspect of life any more. Salacious they may be; politically acceptable, if not exactly correct, they also have to be.

Yet, a very experienced journalist who made the step from *The Times* to *The Sun* found his new title harder to write for than his old. At least in *The Times* you have space to express yourself; in *The Sun*, you have just a few words in which to convey the full meaning of a story. Inevitably, some stories are skimped, but most are represented as believable facts, and are accepted as such at face value by most of their millions of readers.

There is a famous mythical figure in journalistic training circles called Aunty Mary. Aunty Mary is an octogenarian spinster who lives alone in a terraced house in somewhere like Chelmsford, Walsall or Hull. She has a cat, an aspidistra, a fairly basic pension and her health is failing. For the past twenty years the world has passed her by. She has very little idea of the computer age, wouldn't know a fax machine if she saw one, hates new shopping centres, doesn't drive and can't understand why the buses don't run more often, like they used to.

Aunty Mary keeps the television on all the time, for company, not for information. Virtually all the programmes wash over her like visual moving wallpaper and her grasp of news and current events is pretty hazy. There is absolutely no point in blaming Aunty Mary for any of this; it is simply a product of her age, upbringing and level of education. Yet, in some journalist training, all press articles need to be written so that Aunty Mary can not only understand them, but so that she actually wants to read them right through from start to finish. That is a tall order but it is possible and, once achieved, it will greatly improve the clarity and readability of virtually all the documents put out by that particular writer.

Aunty Mary may be the lowest common denominator but she also represents, to a slightly extreme degree, the level for which many internal communications practitioners have to write if they are to grab and retain the interest of their audience. Accordingly there are a few basic rules, shamelessly borrowed from journalism, which can help to achieve this.

Golden Rules

Keep sentences down to no more than twenty words. Flowing Keatsian prose might have been appropriate for a degree in English, but it will be neither appreciated nor understood by the majority of employees.

Write short, simple paragraphs with plenty of white space in between. The copy has to look interesting as well be interesting. Visual breath marks are necessary for most readers, with the possible exception of keen students of Dickens who sometimes stretched a single paragraph over an entire page. Your employees may not appreciate this school of writing.

Say what you've got to say and then shut up. It will gain brownie points galore and avoid all that pompous repetition so beloved of so many editors of in-house journals.

Keep all articles down to five paragraphs. If the topic is really iconoclastic (in which case, what is it doing in an in-house newspaper?) you can go to seven paragraphs, but never any more. This means around 300 words at most; 200-250 is much better; 100-150 is better still. If it cannot be said in this length, then it is probably too ambitious a piece of news to consign to an in-house publication and may need a special document all to itself – or another type of communication medium.

A good journalist will sleep on what he/she has written, if there is time, review it the next morning and question its interest and readability factors. It is important to ensure that it is as topical and interesting as possible. Once this has been ascertained, with the help of a re-write if necessary, the journalist will cut it by 20 per cent, sometimes even by 25 per cent. It will be a better article as a result. That's exactly the same approach taken by TS Eliot with

The Waste Land, except that he asked Ezra Pound to do the reviewing, and the poem has become one of the defining manuscripts of the 20th century.

If the issue is contentious, try to anticipate some of the most common comments and questions that employees are likely to put up by creating a 'Question and Answer' document for line managers. Sometimes, this can be reproduced and printed in an in-house newspaper or even issued to all employees. In the form of short, sharp questions and answers to support a statement about, say, a change in policy, it can give a great deal of information in handily sized bites without alienating or confusing an essentially not highly literate audience.

Remember that, if most people are not highly literate, they are even less numerate. Lots of figures either frighten them or bore them – perhaps both. So keep documents, which necessarily deal with money, such as an employee annual report, to the absolute minimum in terms of technical and monetary speak. Use figures very sparingly and then make sure that you explain exactly what they mean. Many financial editors wish that PR people would do the same.

Ensure that a contact is quoted for responses so that the piece of communication becomes genuinely two-way. Without this element, it cannot be said that the organisation has communicated properly or professionally.

Timing is critical; there's little point in putting out a message long after the rumour machine has already leaked a lurid version of it. Get your clear and simple message out in time to combat the inevitable jungle telegraph.

Even worse is to issue a statement several days after the story has appeared in the local newspaper or been aired on the local radio station. This is almost an insult to employees because it demonstrates just how far down the pecking order they come in terms of management target audiences. As soon as something appears in the media, therefore, try to get a response of some kind into the employee arena. It's hard to achieve, but employees appreciate this and sometimes make allowances. Also, the more practice organisations get, the better they become at it.

Write for the Reader

One very important rule is not to write just what your organisation wants you to say. Don't write for your manager to clear the copy but for your audience to read it. The audience, usually the employees, is the readership that matters; all your manager has to do is to clear the words. His/her task is relatively easy, it's the impact of those words on the employees which is going to determine the success or otherwise of the piece of communication.

It's also important that you don't simply repeat messages that you may not fully understand; question them, interpret them, gain agreement for that interpretation and, only then, issue them. Managers who issue half-understood messages can easily be found out by perfectly innocent questioning on the part of their subordinates. If they don't know the answers, or if they have made up the answers and are then exposed as having done so, it is going to be very difficult for them to regain any credibility.

Find out what the audience believes before you issue anything. Research the feelings, expectations and opinions of the employees, perhaps by commissioning a communications audit from an independent company. This will also provide a treasure chest of information which, if used properly, will help to shape future internal communications strategy as well as the short-term tactical approach to what needs to be said, how, when and to whom.

Remember to listen; writing or speaking is only part of the communication process, the rest is listening, showing you have listened and understood and are taking account of what you've been told in future messages and actions.

Don't make the message fit the media, no matter how high tech, glamorous, existing and seductive a multimedia approach may seem. The media must be suited to the message, not the other way around. Expensive videos/ multimedia packages telling a workforce that their site is to close and their jobs are to go will not be well received no matter how professionally they have been created. Instead, questions will be asked about how much it cost and simple, if misleading, arithmetic about how many jobs the cost of that presentation could have preserved will enter the folklore of the organisation – to its detriment.

Nothing, no matter how glitzy, can replace honest face to face communication. Vauxhall Motors have found that the vast majority of their employees prefer to be addressed in person rather than by a box of tricks. Employees also want to hear information from their own managers in preference to sophisticated, and obviously expensive, technology.

Most importantly, as with press relations, you must have something definite to say before you communicate. There is no point, and much potential damage, in reiterating pulp for the sake of it; that is why so many in-house magazines and newspapers fail so dismally and why, as a concept, they are roughly 50 years out of date. It's not always possible to fill a monthly newspaper with really relevant or readable copy. Sometimes, the organisation simply doesn't generate this interest level and no amount of verbal padding will alter that.

Monitor the success of the message honestly; deceiving yourself, or others, about its success will only pile up problems for the future. If something isn't being well received you have to take that early warning signal and act on it very firmly and very quickly. Otherwise the grapevine rumblings will prevent you from being proactive and you'll simply end up chasing other people's messages and fire fighting.

Be honest; nothing irks employees more than a bland veneer of cheerful twaddle laid over what might be, for them, a deeply disturbing message. Glossy razzmatazz and sales-speak don't impress employees who probably know far more about some aspects of the organisation and its business than you do.

Also, try to ensure a reasonable level of consistency between the external and internal messages. If what you say in an employee communications exercise is in direct conflict with what appeared in the local newspaper two days earlier, you're going to have a lot of very difficult explaining to do to a very unsympathetic audience.

Treat communicating as an integral part of a manager's responsibility – just like budget control. It is not a bolt-on goody or an afterthought; it is a dedicated and demanding discipline.

It requires mental effort, the acquisition of personal communication skills which are foreign to many managers and the shouldering of substantial responsibility for the communication and its consequences. Above all, keep messages short; not everybody wants to read reams of wisdom.

Finally, when creating the short-term communications project or designing the approach to the longer term messages, bear in mind the planning principles we set out before.

- The **objectives** of your communication. What do you want the employees to do, think, say, feel as a result of your communications?

- The **key messages** of the communication. The real meat of the message, stripping away all unnecessary verbiage.

- The **target audiences**. Are you communicating to all employees or only those at one or more locations, or to certain levels of management?

- The **strategy** of how you are going to go about it, whether by personal communications, the written word, videos, etc. Who will head up the effort and which managers will face off to which audiences?

- The **methodology** of what exactly you are going to do, when and through what media. The costed and scheduled details of the exercise.

- The **timescale**, remembering that, once the message has gone out to the first employee, you can no longer keep it confidential in any way or control its ongoing communication – even outside the organisation.

- The **evaluation** of the communications process, running health checks and mini audits from time to time and building into managers' job descriptions responsibility for gaining and delivering feedback.

CHAPTER NINE

The Main Direct Communication Techniques I

The Written Route

Irrespective of the merits or otherwise of the language, there is a large range of written options open to internal communications practitioners and this chapter will look at some of the most common. It will exclude the verbal and modern technology communication routes which will be examined in the following two chapters.

This chapter does not pretend to contain an exhaustive list of internal communication literature, but looks briefly at some of the more common and useful methods of written communication.

Minutes

The first route is one which is not always the first to spring to mind, even with seasoned internal communications specialists. Board/management meeting minutes form the most senior piece of informative paper in any organisation. As such they can be very revealing, very informed and very powerful. The trouble is, they can also be very sensitive.

Seldom, if ever, are they available in their entirety for many members of staff to see, but they do summarise virtually all activities important to the organisation and contain the best news digest available. Some organisations produce bowdlerised versions for further consumption among, for example, second-tier management, but rarely do they go below this level.

This is one instance in which the public sector, especially local government, often has an advantage over the private sector. Council or committee papers are usually open to perusal by all officers and employees of a local authority, with the exception of one or two reserved matters, which are confidential in terms of staff or finance issues. Not many private sector organisations would welcome that kind of openness too often and, in fairness, not many of their staff would always understand or appreciate the information.

Branding the digest of board decisions is another way of extending the use of this device and making it appear to be particularly relevant and readable to its audience. A branded digest is more likely to become a regular point of information than simply copying or e-mailing the minutes of a certain body. To many people, especially in major or complex organisations, the full minutes will mean very little. Most employees are probably not familiar with many of the issues involved, do not understand them and have no desire to do so. A branded digest, however, which simplifies those issues about which something can be communicated, can prove a valuable and highly illuminating document which is likely to create anticipation and a sense of belonging among many employees.

However, the minutes of the governing body of an organisation form the best possible summary of issues that will affect most staff. Consequently, some organisations are moving towards a system in which these minutes can be summarised, de-sensitised and made available for wider inspection than merely the board or committee membership.

Where this can happen without compromising confidentiality, the results can be excellent, but examples of successful practice in this respect in the private sector are rare. One or two brave souls have tried it but the weight of senior management opinion is usually against it. Perhaps it is an ideal to-wards which to work rather than a practical short-term innovation.

Management Briefings

Management briefings usually contain professional information to enable managers to do their jobs better. They may well contain such professional minutiae as statistics on performance, quality, sales, returns, warranty levels, competitors' performance, overseas news, major policy changes and so on.

What they are not designed for is a broad audience. They have identified a sector target audience of management at certain levels and they collate information that helps these managers to do their jobs better. In particular, briefings may help managers to manage their staff better by giving them the latest intelligence on key issues and by suggesting the line to take on questions that may be asked by employees.

Well-planned management briefings can be an invaluable aid to managerial performance. Badly planned and executed bulletins can be an embarrassment. The difference lies, once more, in the planning process. If the audience and its needs and perceptions have been clearly identified, and if the document meets those needs and pays regard to those perceptions, the chances are that the document will become invaluable. If the planning has not been carried out properly, the chances are that the whole exercise will be an unnecessary waste of budget and resource.

Often taking a very modest format, management briefings, which may also be called bulletins, circulars or all sorts of other names, essentially compress information about performance and competition or broader sector trends into a short punchy document. Briefings may make few or little pretensions towards being couched in glittering prose and they certainly will not be confused with the language of a prose writer like Gibbon, but they do the job. Moreover they do the job inexpensively, quickly, regularly and reliably and that is their purpose in life.

Distribution of most management briefings is relatively straightforward in most companies, especially those who now put a briefing on to e-mail, largely because the numbers involved are not high. If the document has any relevance at all, managers should look forward to receiving their briefings each week, very soon clamouring for a missed copy. This, indeed, is the trick of successful management briefings – that they contain a digest of the information which managers need to carry out their jobs properly. Once this balance has been achieved, with as few frills as possible, the exercise is almost certain to be successful.

Not all have small production runs. BT produced *The Manager*, a 24-page, black and white, business magazine published every two months, though the paper version has been superceded by an online publication on the company's intranet. The circulation of the paper version was around 30,000, all within the organisation, which, itself, employs a total of around 130,000. Articles of feature length nestled alongside snippets of industry news or profiles of senior management. Space was devoted to BT's newest developments, individual ideas which were being taken up or results of surveys. A typical contents list of the paper version included the following.

- **Merger update**. BT's vision is alive and well, says Sir Peter Bonfield (CEO).

- **Cegetal's new logo**. Partnership aims for friendlier range.

- **Good and getting better**. BT receives EQA (European Quality) Prize for second year running.

- **Dr Rudge leaves BT**. After more than a decade (as Deputy CEO) on the bridge at BT.

- **Delighting Customers**. Peter Manning's challenge at Concert Customer Service.

- **Learning to lead around the globe**. New programme is first of its kind.

- **European year against racism**. What BT is doing.

- **Counting the cost of poor driving**. Managers urged to drive wisely (significantly contributed by the Head of Group Risk and Insurance).

The preamble to the edition under review points out that *The Manager* was "not to be shown outside BT" (although permission was willingly granted to quote it in outline here) and, certainly, some of the articles might just have given useful news to BT's competitors, of whom there are over 250 in the UK alone. Equally, a good deal of the content would be pretty unintelligible to most lay audiences, so there is a reduced level of risk attached to the majority of the content. It's difficult to avoid the impression that if anything is really top secret, it is not going to be starring in the online version of *The Manager* for a while yet.

Written and edited by CRD (Corporate Relations Department), the magazine was balanced, informed and a trifle worthy, but it worked. Distribution was a well-honed process with a note at the front proclaiming that:

> All BT people are now able to call the Employee Contact Unit (ECU) which provides an online single point of contact to amend their contact details on MERIT, the personnel database. The circulation list of *The Manager* is taken from this database . . . A fax service . . . is available for people who are unable to call during office hours.

Not earth shattering, maybe, but efficient and practical, and it worked.

Employee Bulletins

Management briefings are not to be confused with employee bulletins – regular documents which contain similar information about the company as the management briefing but at a simpler level; if objectively presented without attempting to exhort greater employee effort in every issue, these bulletins can become a useful tool in showing employees the problems facing the organisation and spelling out what they have to do to help. It is not new but remains one of the best devices yet developed and, interestingly, some smaller organisations are now merging this with the management briefing.

This process adds to the unity of the organisation by ensuring that everyone has the opportunity to receive the same information at the same time and in the same form as everyone else. It also saves on creation and production costs, although this is a minor aspect. More importantly, it shows that all employees are being treated as relative equals – and this is one of the great strengths about an employee bulletin.

To take another example, Vauxhall Motors, has a Luton Plant Newsletter, as well as one for the other major plant at Ellesmere Port, which sets out the main aspects of job-based information every week. Thus the two-page, three-colour, newsletter contains sections for a regular update on quality (divided into overall, body, paint, general assembly and parts together with a compound audit), plant performance (in terms of efficiency and bonus payments), a note of long-serving staff, environmental affairs, sales (not just of Luton-based Vauxhalls but of all major players in the UK and broader European markets) and a few miscellaneous items such as new faces, births and deaths, promotions and information on educational facilities available through Vauxhall.

Again, the document is workmanlike, has no pretensions to style and keeps its language, if not exactly simple, at least within the jargon which is understood by most within the motor industry. Distribution again is simple, within a self-contained site, and there is the opportunity to contribute news of fellow employees, miscellaneous aspects and so on through the plant newsletter co-ordinator.

In intellectual terms, this might be seen as a throwback to former days, yet, it works, is simple and is reliable. Also, in many organisations, it is a ready-made vehicle, which could, if necessity arose, be used during difficult times, such as industrial unrest. In that sense, it is worth retaining as a tried and trusted platform in which all employees are seen to be pulling in the same direction, even if they are not.

House Magazines

Now, the moment we've all been waiting for, we come to that favourite old chestnut, the internal newspaper/magazine – regularly produced for all employees and attempting to be a proper publication. Unfortunately, it very seldom is.

Because it too often tries to be all things to all employees, it often tries too hard to rival an external newspaper or magazine. So, the big publications may have space devoted to gardening, fashion, cookery, motoring, sport, social activities and all the rest of the paraphernalia. Some carry advertising from outside bodies – useful to eke out the budget but not necessarily helpful when it comes to keeping the focus on the organisation which is producing it.

Some organisations take a great deal of pride in their in-house newspapers, so much so that it would be quite easy to fill an entire book with an appraisal of their worth. However, as this is not possible here, below are a few of the better examples, and one or two anonymous references to less than good practice.

First, a late and possibly lamented, example of a good magazine aimed at all employees of NatWest Group. Twenty-four pages, full colour, it was called *Agenda* and ran from 1993–1997 being closed because of financial cutbacks. It had a regular digest of what was in the news that affected NatWest, a profile of a senior corporate figure, a section on the local community involvement, another on the customer connection, a business focus feature, a delve into the archives (always a good idea if you're stuck for a page or so) a whole section on people within the group (what they were doing that was newsworthy and why), a regular section called 'On The Move', retirements, pensioners' social calendar, marketplace (essentially, classified ads), staff offers (trips to Walt Disney's World on Ice, staff motor insurance, first day cover stamps and customised tee shirts) and, of course, letters from readers.

And, with minor variations, that format could equally well represent the majority of in-house newspapers or magazines. Some model themselves lavishly on daily papers; *The Vauxhall Mirror*, for instance, even has a masthead that looks like that of *The Mirror*. Again, it packs into its sixteen tabloid pages all the usual areas: industry news, performance landmarks, social stories, competition winners, lottery coupons, news from GM in the US, the environment column, fleet customer profiles, family days out, local community involvement, pensioners' association news, reader offers, computer systems and sports achievements news, lots of classified ads, in memoriam, crosswords, and two main editions, one for Luton and the other for Ellesmere Port. Of its kind, it is a very good example, as you would expect from a company of the stature of GM's UK arm.

Another good example is *BT Today*, winner of countless awards and one of the leading lights in its field. At 24 pages, it uses exceptionally good layout and design as well as writing to make a great deal of otherwise not very palatable material very digestible indeed. Largely about what BT is doing in industrial and developmental terms, it also has space for all kinds of different aspects of life in BT: adverts from finance and car leasing companies, a daughters of employees competition and work day event, a whole section entitled 'Benefits Plus', including 'Privilege Pages', classified ads, news of school governors who are also BT employees, retail news, and lots of news about what employees are doing, why, how, where and to whom. There is very little that anyone could add to *BT Today*. It comes out in various editions to meet the disparate reading needs of all 130,000 employees. A small team plus an external advertising sales agency are kept busy producing this monthly paper which long ago outgrew its affectionate sobriquet of 'BT Toady'.

Finally in the showcase, *Abbey View* for employees of Abbey National – a glossy, full colour 68-page magazine, this one really does the job properly with features on everything you could think of that would be of interest to a bank's customers – and a lot that wouldn't. Satirical coverage of the news, profiles (in the issue under review, the actress Kirstin Scott Thomas and management guru Edward de Bono), an antiques column, a makeover page, cycling in Cuba (for charity, of course) 24 hours in Glasgow, healthy food, environmental issues (again), a horoscope, summer entertainment, a competition to win a helicopter flight and, naturally a piece on the arrival of the euro and what it means to all of us.

Here is probably the most complete magazine for staff that anyone could imagine. It takes a staff of nine to create it once a quarter and it has to take poll position in the in-house mag stakes. If you need a role model, here it is – for now.

However, newspaper or magazine, and we have deliberately looked at a couple of each type, the in-house publication has a number of drawbacks. Firstly, it has to be read before it can do any good. Tautological, but true. Some years ago the management conducted an audit of a very professional in-house newspaper at BL Cars, the *Austin Morris Express*. In style it was based on the daily paper of a similar name, it was written largely by two highly professional journalists who both write for national dailies, had all sorts of contributions from all sorts of people including famous racing drivers and included all the usual gardening, fashion, cookery, crosswords, competitions and so on – just as the titles mentioned above have.

The survey among the target audience showed that, while it might have all these attributes, very few people ever bothered to read it. Great piles of the things were discovered simply gathering dust at the distribution points for weeks after the issue was printed. In internal communications terms, by itself, it was virtually irrelevant.

And that is the main problem with in-house publications of a general nature. In most cases, they have very little impact on the hearts and minds of employees, except, possibly, to alienate them if the front page is full of propaganda. It has another problem in that, as a vehicle for communications, it is static, which is the very thing that vehicles cannot afford to be. Take this introduction to a house journal drawn, at random, from a pile of them.

> . . . the editor will need to be a man of tact, discrimination, energy, fearlessness, caution, subtlety and guile. If perhaps, he does not start with all these qualities he will gain them in the exercise of his new profession . . . The best of luck . . .

Part of an introduction to a newly re-launched in-house magazine for the staff of the then Abbey Road Building Society in – 1930. The words, by the Chairman, Sir (later Lord) Josiah Stamp, come down over the intervening 70 odd years as being just as true today as they were then.

And the content in that issue, too, is remarkably similar. A general manager's preface (admittedly in pompous language which is unlikely to have been read by many and understood by even fewer) a report of the AGM, adverts for goods as diverse as Delysia lingerie, *Ideal Home* magazine, mortgages at 5 per cent and new houses in Golders Green from £695, a notice board page, social news, feature articles on satisfied customers, poems, cartoons, jokes, a calendar for the year including such luminous dates at 12 August ("Grouse shooting begins; rarely a grouse and never any shooting at Abbey House" – quite so), and All Fools Day ("Instituted mainly for non-members of the Abbey Road Society") and even Derby Day (" . . . put your money on the Abbey. It's stable") and more delving into the archives which, even in those days, went back for nearly 60 years.

Apart from the obvious content, and changes of style to accommodate more up to date tastes, there is not too much difference between the feel of that document and a modern day counterpart – and this truth is by no means restricted to Abbey National. One major company's in-house newspaper (not Abbey National's) which recently celebrated its diamond jubilee made great play of the continuity of its approach and style, illustrating this with examples from the mid-1930s. Unfortunately, upon examination, it became fairly clear that the original 1930s editions were significantly superior in terms of writing style, content, layout and interest ratings. Maybe that's not such a good comparison for the proprietors to make, especially as it also boasted a mere five editors over all those years, which makes you wonder whether the job is a fast track, talented, vigorous key management position or a sinecure in the autumnal pastures.

Although, now very old-fashioned, in-house newspapers and magazines are still too often seen as the major communication effort; many managers fail to realise they are a means to a communications end, not an end in itself. If they are part of an integrated internal communications policy, as at BT and Abbey National, for instance, they can have a role to play, albeit a minor one which acts largely as literary wallpaper, much akin to muzak. Without such an integrated policy, they really should be confined to a cage in *Jurassic Park*.

Memos

Memos are not a form of communication that managers readily think about when confronted with internal communications vehicles, but they are probably one of the more widespread method of communicating which are going to happen in any case, although many are now replaced by e-mail which is discussed in a later chapter.

"You've been thrilled by the film, riveted by the book, now marvel at the memo that started it all" is one of the better notepad message that has appeared in recent years. On the whole, far too many memos are written and sent; personal visits to neighbouring offices or phone conversations would often be much more productive, far less political and less prone to misinterpretation.

It is difficult to avoid the impression that memos are often used by many inadequate managers as a shield behind which to hide. There was a flagrant case of two public sector managers squabbling over who should have access to the office mobile phone in the mid-1990s. It was all conducted by memo through two long-suffering and unnecessarily put-upon secretaries and it became very vindictive, personally abusive and extraordinarily petty – all over a mobile phone.

What was needed was either for the two managers to grow up and talk out their problems with each other face to face, or, in the continuing absence of any sign that they were going to do so, for their director to force them to do it. In the end, the secretaries came to an amicable agreement and presented the two inadequate managers with a *fait accompli*. Nevertheless, it was a blatant waste of time, money and clerical resources. Sadly, it is probably typical of many organisations in which civilisation seems to break down in the face of life's basic needs, such as mobile phones.

There is also no question that a number of middle and senior managers have attained their current levels because they have cultivated the knack of writing very good memos. Whether they are any good at anything else is a moot point. One such director, in the private sector, this time, was quite brilliant at the art form and could either stir up or calm down a situation almost unerringly with a few well-considered memos tactically copied in to various managers, directors and others. Unfortunately, after nine years, his ability to do the actual job for which he was getting paid became open to question and his very senior position (Director of International Marketing for a large multinational) was summarily and very bloodily terminated. Even then, his ability to put together convincing memos lasted long enough for him to obtain a very handsome, tax free settlement.

If, however, the political element can be reduced in memo writing, and it can probably never be eliminated altogether, the vehicle itself is useful. Of necessity short and sweet, a memo should convey to the interested parties exactly and succinctly what is going on and what is expected of whom, a bit like a contact report. When viewed in this light, and when the discipline is tightened up to prevent personal crusades and overt politicking, the humble memo has its place.

Notice Boards

Practical, workaday utilities, such as notice boards, electronic bulletin boards and other places of public notice or address, which can communicate useful, if basic, information to groups of employees, also have their place. These form a cumbersome and often neglected aspect of internal communications, which needs to be properly organised and policed to avoid it becoming like a newsagent's window.

One accurate way of assessing the worth of an organisation is to examine the notice boards visible on the way to and from meeting rooms. If they are messy, uncontrolled, open to all sorts of adverts for holidays in Spain, second-hand Skodas, baby sitting and slightly used prams, the organisation is likely to follow similar lines.

If they show signs of having been policed regularly, with special areas set aside for different categories of notice (health and safety, unions, organisational information, social, educational and departmental) then it's a fair chance that the organisation is similarly well organised and can put its hand on most of the files it might need for your meeting. This is not, however, a foolproof measure of efficiency and should not be taken too far. It might just mean that somebody has the unenviable job of maintaining the notice board, but that he or she might do very little else.

Letters

One method of communicating which certainly has its place is the direct personal letter, usually from the CEO or a locally based director to individual employees. Sometimes it is delivered to homes, so that families can read the letter as well, giving the benefit of exerting another pressure on the employee – that of family opinion.

This device can be extremely effective for announcements of major importance but, because of this, should be used very sparingly, no more than twice a year, or they lose their effect. They also need to be short, sweet and to the point because they are trespassing on home territory; courtesy and common sense dictate that this intrusion should be kept as brief as possible and not outstay its welcome.

Sometimes, the very presence of the letter is unwelcome anyway, but, if that is the case, the chances are that the organisation has already lost the respect and confidence of the workforce to some degree. Accordingly, a rather more radical measure than a photocopied letter is probably called for.

Direct letters to homes can be very effective in times of industrial dispute, especially strikes in which attitudes have hardened and any appeal to the strikers themselves is likely to be rejected with affront. Appealing to the spouse, partner and family, however, is one way of circumnavigating the attitude issue and will be looked at in the chapter on indirect communication.

Information Packs

Sometimes, there is a need to create and issue a full spectrum of information about a major topic, in which case information packs can be used, usually in conjunction with a major change in something fundamental to employees' lives, such as working practices, site closure or relocation. Again, this device is most effective when used sparingly; the last thing employees want to see is yet another glossy fat wad of information which probably cost as much as their salary. If it comes out once in a blue moon, however, it is more likely to be appreciated; management has taken time, trouble and effort in order to express the organisation's point of view and, therefore, probably cares what its employees think.

This is not to be confused with an induction pack which, too often, looks like a KGB manual of practice outside which it may be fatal to stray. Beloved of HR staff, as though they were the golden bough of inculcation into an organisational culture, induction packs are too easily dismissed as lightweight, procedural manuals which are there to tell people how to behave and what not to do. Approached with a modicum of intelligence they are capable of doing vastly more, including indicating how new incumbents can integrate into the organisation they have joined, for richer or poorer.

They can, for example, point out not just what to do and what not to do but where things are, who looks after what, who to talk to when your immediate manager or supervisor is not around and, perhaps, equally advisable, who not to talk to. Student unions have been doing good work in this regard for decades; given that many graduates go on to become managers, why this skill cannot be translated more consistently into organisational induction manuals is an unfathomable mystery. As with most aspects of internal communications, some organisations, of course, do it very well, others barely pay regard to basic legal requirements and make little or no attempt to inject an element of helpful humanity into the project.

Guidelines

Instruction guidelines of various kinds, mainly related to how you carry out your job, are also opportunities to communicate with an employee in a way which he/she is unlikely to ignore at the tender stage of early exposure to the organisation. Here is the chance to set out not just what needs to be done but why, what effect it can have on other employees, what overall contribution that job makes to the organisational effort and how the rewards of satisfaction and enhancement can follow as result.

Interestingly, one local authority, which comes in for praise in this regard, has had the foresight to develop a basic version of an information pack for both the deaf and the blind, the latter being executed in braille. It is, necessarily, rather more limited than the full pack, but, nevertheless, it attempts to put itself into the mind of those at whom it is aimed (with the aid of blind or deaf employees) and provides information which is of special value and interest to them. Since it is not too often that local authorities can claim to be blazing the shining pioneering trail, especially in communications terms, this innovation ought to be given due credit and applauded for its courtesy.

Employee Reports

Finally, employee annual reports are often well worth the relatively small effort involved. They usually contain most of the meat of the full annual report without the financial detail and are expressed in rather more reader-friendly language than is usually to be found on the Stock Exchange.

They do, however, convey the key aspects of life in an organisation, especially how well it is doing and whether there will be a job for most employees in twelve months, as well as details of compelling pecuniary interest, such as bonus payments; can you afford that new carpet or not?

The usual suspect areas are covered, such as the chairman's report, inevitably but rather more relevantly than usual. If the chairman cannot talk to his/her employees at annual report and results time, there is something wrong – probably the organisation's communications policy. The results would not have been possible without the employees, maybe they could be a great deal better next time with more employee involvement, so this is a natural juncture at which to make this point, usually in conjunction with a personal presentation, if that is feasible.

Employee annual reports also include aspects of interest such as where the growth (or the decline) came from, how the individual companies or divisions are performing, how the organisation is interacting with the environment and its local communities and how and where it is investing in new plant, technology, systems and skills. Above all, how the organisation relates to its people is one of the most important aspects of any employee annual report and results.

One example emanating from the, then, eighth biggest British company manages to get on one sparsely written side of A3 all its activities on the community, environment, health and safety and equal rights (no less than eight lines, or 47 words, on this last topic). It could be that this is a classic example of concise prose; it could equally be that the organisation merely paid lip service to '-isms' and other aspects of life which it regarded as disagreeable, irrelevant or irritating – or even all three. Certainly, its share value has fallen by nearly 75 per cent in the last ten years (even discounting the effects of inflation) and it is difficult to dissociate that fall from grace with the conspicuously meagre approach to communications, both internal and external, which that organisation has traditionally espoused. Unfortunately, it is now probably too late to reverse the trend, but by being held up as a beacon of inadequate communications, it might, at least, help to prevent similar fates befalling other organisations. Two short quotations from this report may heighten the irony. The first is attributed to the then chairman.

> As standards of living escalate, the needs of society, perceived and real, increase. Our opportunities to satisfy those needs multiply, as do those for the creation of wealth for shareholders, employees and customers. These opportunities were well taken in 19—.
>
> As we move towards the next decade, there are many reasons for believing that we will maintain that record into the future. Growth is the goal, profit the measure, security the result.

Sanctimonious expressions and clichés like this will work for a time; they may even last for a few years, but, sooner or later they will be found out if they are not substantiated by results and sound performance. This is a classic case of over writing the bull and not underwriting the business.

CHAPTER TEN

The Main Direct Communication Techniques II

The Verbal Route

This chapter does not pretend to be an exhaustive list of verbal communication techniques but one that looks briefly at some of the more common and useful methods of communicating in verbal terms.

Cascades

The first technique to mention, and one of the best known to most practitioners of the art, is the cascade system. In theory, this starts the communication process at the top and the message then magically flows down through the organisation. It has a number of advantages, notably that of empowering managers to communicate directly to their own section of employees, thereby enhancing their own credibility and putting an appropriate interpretation on the corporate message.

It is, or should be, automatic, fast and well proven. Sometimes it is, sometimes, it isn't. In theory there is no reason why the cascade system, once firmly established, cannot operate smoothly each time the need occurs. Indeed, sometimes, there may be a case for calling together employees even when there isn't anything particularly dramatic to impart simply to carry on the tradition of cascading meetings and raising, and fulfilling, expectations of regular communications.

Cascades need to be quick, accurate and sensitive. Their natural enemy is the predatory jungle telegraph and it is unlikely that any officially structured system can really ever beat this unofficial rumour machine. With care, planning and the willing co-operation of managers, however (especially the latter) it is possible to match the telegraph and to go further than it can, because the cascade is based on informed intelligence rather than rumour. Thus the confirmation or otherwise of a rumour is something which the cascade system does have in its power, and that is an important advantage which can help to colour employee reaction to its very existence.

But to stand any chance at all, the system has to be able to react very quickly. Sometimes it also has to be able to predict the need for a particular message to be cascaded and set up the system at very short notice on the strength of managerial probability. This is an eventuality with which many managers, especially in HR realms, feel less comfortable and can be a drawback to cascading. It is all very well to set up a cascade system that can roll into operation at known times (say, at annual results time) but to create one which can be flexible enough to operate smoothly at the drop of a hat (as in the case of, say, a takeover) is a much more difficult operation. It can be done, but only in organisations which have a strong culture of internal communications, responsible middle managers who are used to communicating and have been trained in it and senior managers who are very open about what they are, and are not, doing. That series of qualifications effectively removes many organisations from the list of those that can operate a genuinely effective cascade system under almost any circumstances.

Accuracy is another principle for cascade systems; if they cannot be accurate they are worse than useless. Their chief merit is that they are communicating the gospel, not a rumour, but the truth. Take away that element and they have no more credibility than any other rumour insidiously pervading the organisation. In fact, they can do a great deal of damage in the credibility stakes because, if they are proven to be inaccurate, they will put back the cause of employee trust in management utterances for a very long time and probably undo a lot of good work which many people have laboured long and hard to create.

Similarly, they have to be not just sensitive but seen to be sensitive. Charging around like a bull in a china shop is not a recommended approach to internal communications at the best of times. When it is carried out in an official way (i.e. through official managers who use official communications channels), it has to be hyper-sensitive and demonstrably so, otherwise clumsiness of the individual can be rapidly translated by an anxious workforce as being clumsiness of the entire managerial structure within the organisation. This might, of course, be the case but, if so, it is better not to admit the fact.

There is also the cliché of the cascade system that responds to a rumour or other situation with too little information too late. One medium-sized engineering company was recently relocating a number of its operations and, partly because of complications with the property deals and partly because the management was singularly inept in communicating in any case, it allowed all sorts of rumours to grow about the future of one location or another and the consequent uncertainty which hung over some jobs. In fact, no job losses were threatened because the new locations were all very close to the existing ones but, because the managers didn't bother to state this, the jungle telegraph had a field day.

The upshot of it all was that, by the time the final announcements did come and managers took their teams aside to tell them the plan of action for relocation, several resignations had already been filed and accepted, as key people moved to competitors, and the atmosphere was of such suspicion that much of what was said was not believed in any case. This was exacerbated because the managers were not permitted to tell all the details, which many of them did not know anyway. The consequent half-truths, uncertainties, hesitations and side-steppings were interpreted by the employees as being devious and dishonest, symptomatic of even greater evil to come. The trickle of resignations became a stream and, long before the final relocation, there was a major recruitment crisis in the company, mainly in key areas of skilled workers who knew they could get equally good jobs with more reliable organisations if they went to work for competitors. At a conservative estimate, it took that company two years to overcome the effects of this lack of clear, open communication about an issue, which should have had virtually no negative connotations and many positive ones.

Another aspect of cascade systems is that they can be relatively rigid in that managers tend to pass on messages parrot fashion unless guideline notes are used allowing greater freedom of interpretation – but this can lead to misinterpretation. There is a fine line between how far organisations wish to tell the message in the same way to all employees and how far they want to let individual managers have some leeway to interpret the message within the context of their particular sections. Do you insist that only the strict form of words is used, which is what some organisations do, or do you give managers the outlines and let them interpret accordingly?

Pragmatic Approach

The answer, as usual, differs from one organisation to another. However, there is danger in either extreme. Too rigid a message is sometimes unintelligible or provokes more questions than it answers, which annoys everyone involved in the cascade process because they think they are being treated like dummies, possibly with some justification. Too little control allows all sorts of fairy tales to be woven by hyper imaginative managers out to fly kites on their own behalf because, if they tell a version of facts which wishfully glamorises their own importance, they may be able to turn the resulting beliefs into reality and claim extra seniority as a *fait accompli*. That is an old trick and it still works tolerably well, especially in organisations which are naturally naive and whose senior management trust their middle management layers too far. Unfortunately, after a few instances of this, they tend to trust them so little that the whole cause of cascaded communications is put back by a few decades.

Cascade systems are also not as widely used in British organisations as some of these organisations would have you believe. Many managers will tell you they have a cascade system in place and they might have, but they seldom entrust it to communicate anything of great importance. In this case, it cannot be said to be a live and fully developed system

Part of the problem here seems to be that, within organisations, some senior managers still liken knowledge to power and are reluctant to part with it. As we have seen elsewhere, once information has been passed to certain managerial levels, they are often very reluctant to pass it on down the line to lesser levels, in case their own advantage of surprise and timely knowledge is eroded. The Duke of Wellington is credited, probably apocryphally, with the old saying:

> Twice armed the man who has his quarrel just
> Thrice armed the man who gets his blow in fust.

Try that one in the boardroom or the management meeting sometime.

The only solution to this problem, and even this won't always work, is to introduce a system of checks and safeguards so that managers who do not communicate know that they will be discovered and exposed as a result. This calls for a strong corporate communications function having the benefit of the friendly and very co-operative ear of the very top managers, which is not a very common occurrence.

The other supposed solutions to the problem are to try to get everyone to imagine everyone else as their customers and to communicate with care, understanding and clarity as a result. Perhaps the best example of the smooth workings of this is the British National Health Service. Another would be the train operating companies. Almost any external customer of these veritable towers of Babel could tell at a glance that the internal communications were almost non-existent and that the successes undoubtedly achieved depend far more on individual heroics and the collective Dunkirk spirit than on any form of cohesive internal communications.

Conducting an internal communications survey for one health trust, a communications consultancy encountered a hospital that, until very recently, stored its medical and patient records in a disused lift shaft. Not the urgent ones, of course, it would be both improper and silly to suggest that. The urgent ones are kept in a series of supermarket trollies in a disused corridor at the back of the building. Unfortunately, the windows have nearly all been broken, either by vandals or by desperate medical secretaries and rain tends to spoil medical records quite quickly. One of the first and most horrified recommendations of the survey was to computerise the whole records system, but that turned out not to be too popular with some factions who either had a Luddite attitude to computers, or a vested interest in the provision of quill pens to doctors, nurses, surgeons and anaesthetists.

Variation in managers' communications skills can prove a major drawback in the cascade system, especially in larger organisations. Here, again, training can help but it cannot always be more than a short-term palliative for some managers who will never get the hang of the thing. For others, it is a help, although one suspects that the finest help of all is plenty of practice in communicating positive information to responsive listeners.

Presentations

The second major method of verbal communication and one which is very powerful when correctly used, is the presentation direct to the workforce – the place at which this book started over twenty years ago. These can be very appealing and effective, but can also be unwieldy and a nightmare to organise.

For a start, they have to be fitted into a very busy manager's diary and it is unusual for him/her to have enough consecutive free days to carry out all the presentations in one seamless programme. Nevertheless, it is important that this is achieved if possible, otherwise the rumour machine will fasten on to all sorts of half-heard statements from the first presentation and pass these on to other locations with varying degrees of lurid embroidery. Consequently, when the presenter finally arrives at the last location, the whole of what he is going to say (and a great deal that never entered his mind) has already become common knowledge and either accepted wisdom or a reviled creed, depending on circumstances.

In this case, either the employees' expectations are going to be disappointed or they are going to be exceeded, often by a considerable margin in either case. While erring one way is not likely to be a massive problem, erring the other way could be. Consequently, the more consecutive the presentations, the better for all concerned.

Direct presentations can sometimes involve treading on line managers' toes if delivered by senior corporate management and handled insensitively. This may sound silly but some directors and managers can grow very possessive about their locations; they see the operation in which they are in charge as a kind of personal fiefdom and, while this might engender care and responsibility, it can be a nuisance for corporate management. Jaguar Cars during the period 1968-1986, for example, never really thought of itself as part of BL Cars and that lead to many spats, some of them unseemly in their public airing. These could and should have been avoided with better and more sensitive management from both sides, but it is easier to write that in a book than it is to drive it through on the ground.

Often the best compromise is to empower line managers to deliver presentations on behalf of senior corporate managers – after having created the presentations centrally to ensure that the party line is adhered to and that there is no excuse for a declaration of UDI. One way of doing this is with scripted slides, by which a local manager delivers the slide presentation with a commentary that has been provided. This may also have a detailed 'Question and Answer' section to help him/her deal with the questions which will inevitably arise and which are one of the most valuable parts of direct presentations.

Conventional and old-fashioned though this might seem to be, it retains some merit, especially for more traditional organisations. One of the advantages is that it is simple and relatively foolproof – although there is always the odd manager who seems intent on derailing the system, especially in a remote part of the organisational empire.

Another benefit is that it delivers strong corporate speak through the mouthpiece of the local manager, which is almost the ideal situation for many circumstances combining, as it does, the overall leadership's stance on important issues and, probably, relevant intelligence new to the audience, with the underlying authority of the local manager who embodies the organisation in that territory.

The content of such presentations has largely been dealt with in other chapters. However, to re-cap, all professional presentations need a beginning, a middle and an end, with the first and last sections supporting each other by stating and re-stating the single major message of the presentation. More than one major message is usually a waste of time because the second message can become obscured in the first.

Typically, a presentation will have an introduction stating why the presenter is there and what he/she is going to talk about. Then he/she talks about it, preferably using as many visual aids as possible. No audience, no matter how bright, will give a speaker its full attention for more than twelve minutes, unless that speaker is using visual aids: overhead or 35mm slides, Powerpoint slides, video, or even a flip chart, a white board and a few other props. They all make a difference, so much so that, with visual aids, the attention span stretches to seventeen minutes. That's still not very long; just compare it with all those interminable double periods at school or dry lectures at university. But it's long enough in which to make the major point and to sell yourself as a human presenter and manager, one who is willing to meet employees on their own ground.

Thereafter, another fifteen to twenty minutes for questions and answers, depending on how brave the presenter is feeling, will do as much good as the rest of the presentation put together, because it gives employees a chance to air their own views and seek clarification on points which are key to them, although these points might seem unimportant to the originators of the presentation.

Pulsed tapes and pre-recorded videos achieve the same ends, although both are now well behind the front-line of technology. Both can work well, however, are flexible and simple to use and probably are less likely to be defeated by computer illiterates or problems like uncertain power supply.

Video conferencing is not yet the panacea for all ills, although it's trying hard. At the time of writing, technical limitations still have to be overcome if the picture quality is to be improved to satisfactory levels, and it is a good idea to be able to see the colour of your colleagues' eyes. Also, video conferencing is not yet markedly popular with the breed of manager who has traditionally enjoyed an element of luxury travel and accommodation as part and parcel of his/her job. A couple of hours on a box of tricks in the conference room is not as glamorous or appealing as a Concorde flight to New York with, maybe, a day's golf afterwards. This trait is inconvenient for the cost watchers, but very human.

Reviews

Formal reviews, of individuals at regular intervals, are one of the finest methods yet invented for improving the confidence of employees on a one to one basis. They allow for all kinds of grievances and issues to be raised and dealt with in confidence. In turn, this process instils confidence in the employee, or it should do if the manager has anything remotely resembling interpersonal skills. This, in its turn, can be infectious in its effect; allowing other employees to see that a colleague is contented is a first class way of suggesting, subliminally, that there may be a case for them, too, to be contented.

As with many other types of communication, however, managers cannot be expected to be able to carry out successful reviews without specialised training. Many managers are awkward not just about the review process but about asking for help and training if they feel that they need it. Consequently, this is an area in which the HR function really can make a difference with a tactful but firm stipulation that all managers have refresher courses to keep abreast of new developments or new legislation. Some managers protest that they do this in any case and many do it very capably. On the other hand, there are so many disaffected employees in so many organisations that there must be room for improvement in some cases.

The process is a real management discipline with responsibility on both sides to carry out an honest and constructive review that addresses, warts and all, any shortcomings which may be appearing on the horizon. Reviews are not just about the managed but also about the effectiveness of those who manage the managed. This can be perceived as a threat to status, professional reputation and even careers in extreme cases, usually by those managers who are not very good at carrying out reviews. While that may be unfortunate, it is a difficulty that cannot be allowed to stand in the way of good management practice. If the manager will respond to training and review by his/her own boss, all well and good. If not, is he/she the right person to be in that manager's position? Often, the answer is in the negative. After all, if the manager cannot manage the people who report directly to him/her, then the management skills are probably gravely lacking.

Formal or informal talks between managers and a small group of subordinates allow relaxed discussion of issues often best not addressed in public. Such group meetings do, however, rely heavily on the communications skills of the manager concerned, which can sometimes be interesting, especially in the subjective interpretation of information. They can also be vulnerable to inference and lack of clarity as well as politicking.

That is not to say that they do not have a place, and an important one at that, in the make-up of any successful organisation. They reinforce the authority of the manager as the first point of contact for both information and the application of that information for the unit and employees, which he/she manages. This alone can create a confidence in the manager on the part of his/her reporting employees; indeed, without this confidence, the manager may not be perceived to be managing very well.

One thing is certain, no manager can afford to make a mess of a group meeting. This is one occasion for which the preparation must be very thorough and the command of information authoritative, otherwise, any scepticism on the part of employees will be magnified and, perhaps, distorted to the detriment of the manager. Preparation, therefore, which takes into account all the most difficult scenarios that could possible arise is likely to be of substantial benefit. Apart from that perverse law of the universe, which says that, if you prepare for something, it probably won't happen while, if you don't prepare, it almost certainly will, there is a benefit in preparing. Maybe it forces you to brush up on a topic that you had always meant to do but had always put off. Maybe it simply helps you to understand your staff and their feelings and points of view better. Perhaps it even makes you focus on the real issues rather than the perceived ones.

In execution, group meetings are like mini presentations and all the rules must be observed in terms of structure and public, or group, speaking techniques. Small groups can be pitiless in their studying of a manager's foibles, be they mannerisms, speech defects, lack of confidence, appalling dress sense or even body odour or halitosis. And, the more bored they become, the more they are going to study these foibles. Unfortunately, it is these aspects which make a lasting impression and, true to the halo effect, the negative aspects make a far deeper impression than the positive ones. So, you must be absolutely sure, absolutely confident and absolutely secure in group meetings and the only way to achieve this is to prepare, prepare, and then prepare. The former world squash champion, Jonah Barrington, often makes the point that the amateur practises until he gets it right but the professional practises until he cannot get it wrong. Managers need to be professionals.

So, set the agenda and stick to it. Tell everyone what is going to be discussed, put a time limit on it and stick to that time limit. Predetermine what you are prepared to give way on and what you're not and stick to that. Try either to involve everyone or at least ensure that everyone has a chance to air their views. Structure the discussion and chair it sympathetically but firmly. Remember that some aspects of the meeting, which you might think are trivial, can be very important to other people, so don't squash their feelings. Give the group some freedom and they will probably respond more positively to you as a manager when they see that you are prepared to trust them and to treat them as grown ups.

Walkabouts

Walkabouts can also be productive. Simply expressed, they consist of a senior manager taking advantage of a meeting at a location, which they visit fairly infrequently to walk round the site and show their face to the employees. This can work in most situations, offices, factory, warehouse, research unit, workshop, anywhere where employees are carrying out work for the organisation. They are particularly effective in the more distant outposts of an empire where corporate directors or centrally based senior managers seldom stray.

Here, senior figures can do much for employee commitment just by appearing, walking round and asking a few interested questions. It reminds employees that they have not been forgotten, reassures them that someone is interested in what they are doing and that there is a part, possibly a large part, of the organisation for which they work outside their own gates.

The walkabout is the simplest internal communications device yet invented (thousands of years ago) and remains the most underused. At The Body Shop, Anita Roddick walks the shop floor nearly every day and knows the names of all 500 staff in that location. If a greater number of senior managers followed her lead, there might be a greater feeling of belonging and commonality of purpose in many organisations.

Management Meetings

Seminars, workshops and away days are often held in many organisations, predominantly for managers. They can be very effective if handled sensitively. If not, they can be divisive and result in antagonistic views being spread like wildfire.

The key to most away day type events is that they need to be focused on a theme or issue. Merely to gather together a group of managers or other employees and expect the event to go with a swing is futile. Such unfocused events can be embarrassing, counter-productive and highly destructive to the process of team building, especially if they are held at weekends when many employees would far rather be doing something else.

There was, in the 1980s, a rather odd process reminiscent of clutching at straws in this whole team building area. Groups of unsuspecting employees would be rounded up like sheep and whisked off to some paint ball farm or go-karting arena in the name of building better relationships and a greater oneness. Sometimes they may have worked, but the number of paint ball, war games and go-kart facilities appears to have dropped off dramatically throughout the 1990s, so it may be that this fad has had its day.

As a piece of social relaxation, such events are fine and can be amusing, entertaining and fun. As a method of bonding they have a more dubious pedigree and a distinctly indifferent success rate. As a foundation stone of management thinking and training they are seriously flawed and very limited. As an expression of management philosophy and an exponent of management communication, they are rubbish.

Group Meetings

Another method which goes under various names in different organisations but is fundamentally the same, is focus groups, team briefings, diagonal slice or cross functional meetings. These are all kinds of meetings of various focused groups, which are all useful in helping to provide the facility for two-way communication. By dealing in relatively small numbers of employees, they also make the numerical aspect of communicating more manageable – introducing the ability to get one's arms around the tree, as the saying has it.

They are also particularly useful in organisations whose employees tend to be more highly powered (professional and financial services, computer related and so on) because they allow a reasonable measure of input from all members and this often appeals to more highly skilled and educated employees who need to feel that their point of view is being taken into account. By carefully constructing them, these groups can be representative of a broad cross section of the organisation, which is another bonus.

On the other side of the coin, they can, if chosen without due care and attention, end up running the manager ragged and resemble a party political conference more closely than an internal focus group. Clearly, this is not the intention and it behoves those who organise them to have the detailed knowledge of the employees concerned to ensure that those who are particularly self-opinionated, and they exist in every organisation, are matched by firm but sensitive managers who have been properly trained in communications and facilitation skills and who have the experience to cope – as well as the patience of Job.

There are a number of variations on these half dozen main themes, notably the semi-social event with the managing director or another senior figure. Often these tend towards the working breakfast or lunch with some kind of briefing thrown in for good measure rather than simply a social get together. Used properly they can be very effective – for those who attend. Like conferences for the top 100 (or 500, 1000, etc.) managers, they are useful in cascade terms, but only if you find yourself invited. For those who are not, they can be a serious shower of cold water. However, they reflect the hierarchy and can enhance employees' ambitions to be included next time, so they can have a back-door motivational element at times.

Rotating Meetings

A variant of the walkabout occurs when an area management team rotates its meetings to appear in a different part of the organisation each time. This is really only useful if it closes the logical loop by making time to spend with some of the employees in that area, either on an individual or a group basis. Then it can be very effective in showing the flag, although it may be that detailed points are smartly fielded to someone more specialised than the members of the management team. If they were not, the managers would hardly be members of the management team.

One large multinational with locations across eight or nine countries makes a habit of taking it in turns to host the monthly board meeting. Each office, therefore, hosts at least one meeting a year. The result is a workforce who, though highly disparate in nationality, outlook and needs, recognises most of the directors and appreciates the fact that they visit this particular location at least annually. It doesn't appreciably add to costs since all the directors are forever flying all over the world in any case, but it does focus attention on a different location and that is good for two-way communication and understanding.

Mentoring

Mentoring, too, is on the increase and has a great deal to offer – if it is carried out properly. Even high fliers can have uncertainties in making career or managerial choices and the presence of someone a little more senior who has been through similar experiences can often be a subtle and welcome guiding hand.

The system is usually voluntary from both points of view, although professional monitoring consultants are appearing on the open market very rapidly. The senior manager, the mentor, must not be in direct line of command over the junior manager, otherwise the double axis of reporting relationships clouds the issue. The mentor needs to be available for a drink, a meal or a piece of ad hoc advice, rather than making firm and fixed appointments. He/she is more of an agony aunt than a manager but the areas of discussion are usually career or work-related, at least to start with.

Companies as successful as Arthur Andersen and Asda run mentoring systems with quiet success, citing benefits as creating a more open and friendly working environment, providing someone to stimulate thought rather than provide all the answers and providing a respected and trusted friend with whom one can share concerns or triumphs with equal confidence.

Mentoring is not about training or coaching but about confidence building and is the logical extension of the guardian angel type of scheme that runs so well in many good schools. It can be particularly useful for female employees who find themselves up against the infamous glass ceiling. Talking to people who have already managed to break through its prism bars can give them great encouragement and the area looks like being one of the modest but steady growth professions of the early part of the 21st century.

Road Shows

Road shows are often part and parcel of the direct presentation but can be held independently and can also create a very significant impact. Care has to be taken to strike the right balance of information, professionalism and miserliness so that employees don't see the road show as a good deal of budget going up in dry ice. Jobs are too scarce and security of tenure too elusive to risk that kind of accusation.

However, they can bring a sense of drama and motivation to even the dullest section of an organisation, if they are imaginative and focused on the sector they visit. The impervious or insensitive road show, which carries on regardless of the make-up of this week's audience, is likely to fail, even though it may need to create a consistent message across the whole organisation. The art here is to convey the message in slightly different forms so that it appeals in a stronger way to each specialist area. Even changing that part of the presentation which impacts on the particular audience can be enough to persuade them that is not just a piece of PR puffery but a sincere attempt to address employees with relevant information and carefully thought out arguments on relevant issues.

Remember, though, that road shows are expensive in time, budget and resources. Often organisations bring in external companies to organise and produce them, and the level of specialist expertise required for an ambitious road show is such that this is almost inevitable. But some member of staff has to accept overall responsibility and, because of the budget levels and relatively high risk factors, it needs to be someone at middle management stage. He/she will probably have to relinquish most other responsibilities while the road show is being prepared and executed.

The physical as well as managerial disruption can be considerable and it's amazing how many electricians, carpenters, tea ladies and security staff you need at each venue. Often, sets are constructed and commissioned overnight; this involves wages or fees for working unsociable hours and that can amount to a considerable sum. Technical glitches are the norm rather than the exception and the problem always seems to require yet more money throwing at it. Employees can see that this is costing money and reaction can vary from bewilderment to anger or, occasionally, when all goes well, gratification that they are being given the red carpet treatment. For all these reasons, it is as well to try to create the road show for other purposes, perhaps external communications, and to take advantage of it being set up to invite employees to a special showing. This is particularly effective in new product and service launches when, with a bit of luck, the marketing department will cover most of the cost.

Surgeries and Forums

Information surgeries can also be highly successful in taking the information to the employee in a painless and attractive manner. Widely used by the Royal Mail among others, they effectively put the team in charge of a particular project into a room for a given period of time, such as a day, and invite employees at that location to visit at their own leisure to gain further information about that project. This takes the mountain to Mohammed but also allows an element of informality to take charge and should place the exchange of information process on a more informal footing. The project staff will need to be trained in good communications skills on a personal level and may need to rotate, since these events can be very time consuming. However, the investment should be well worthwhile and, the more success that attends the early surgeries, the more eagerly awaited will be the coming of the team to subsequent locations.

Communications forums in which staff take coffee with a selection of senior managers to talk over a range of subjects are also sometimes employed. Similar to some of the ideas above, they can be very wide ranging; indeed, their main drawback is that they can be too wide ranging. Nervous senior managers will fight shy of these on the basis that there are some topics which are not yet in the employee arena, but that is always going to be the case. Nevertheless, properly conducted by confident senior managers, they can be a major influence on their audiences, usually for the better.

Finally, there is the 'grapevine' the natural and implacable enemy of the internal communications practitioner. It can never be beaten and very seldom equalled for speed, information and, above all, its compelling interest factor. Very clever managers can harness it to their own purposes by seeding rumours with particularly well-placed and gregarious staff, but this is a very delicate operation and not often successful in unskilled hands. It can backfire very easily and is not recommended to anyone faint of heart, unfamiliar with the works of Machiavelli or ambitious for a pension. But it can be done and will be looked at in the chapter on indirect methods.

CHAPTER ELEVEN

The Future Perfect and the Combined Approach

Although the written and verbal routes are still the most popular forms of internal communications, it may be that, in a few years, this is not the case and that these have both been overtaken by the convenience and greater flexibility of more modern methods. As people generally read less and less and as faster communications methods become more accessible, more affordable and more convenient, the chances are that they will become the standard by which to judge the forms of communication.

There are a number of communication methods which come into this category and, while few of them are radical, all of them offer alternative, and what might be loosely termed technological, methods of communicating.

E-mail

E-mail is now one of the most widely used methods by which to communicate both internally and externally. It is very convenient, not expensive once the main system has been installed, gives immediate communications to a wide range of addressees and allows instant replies. Similar schemes, such as Lotus Notes, may not last because of the trend towards standardisation; we could see a situation similar to that which afflicted the video market in the early-1980s in which one standard becomes the accepted industry norm to the virtual exclusion of all others.

E-mail, however, still has to have its human input. It is not a robotic process, which automatically logs on to a message and sends it out without recourse to a human manager, although those days may not be far off for some routine communications. For the moment, however, the e-mail still has to be managed and activated by human input – and that makes it just as susceptible to human error as any other system.

Legion are the stories about employees going into work after a few days away and finding several hundred e-mail messages waiting for them, many of no relevance and most of no interest either. This is one of the drawbacks of the system; that it still has to be policed humanly and that much duplication is taking place. It is possible to spend many happy or frustrating hours, wading through messages about cars for sale, baby sitting, management dictats on car parking and currency difficulties in Kazakhstan without ever doing any real work. Dumping has to be ruthless, regular and rational if the system is to be made to serve the users properly rather than run their lives and waste their time.

There are all sorts of debates about the virtues and vices of e-mail, very few of which are actually about the system but more about the people who run the systems. If you get too much mail, it is hardly the system's fault. If the system misses you out, it is probably because nobody thought to tell it you existed. If the list of addresses is incorrect, it is probably because nobody thought to update it. These are all human fallibilities, which are common to all sorts of communication systems, be they electronic or based on the carrier pigeon. The system is only as good as its human managers – for now. This observation is equally true when aimed at the other electronic and modern age systems with which the modern office is increasingly equipped.

Also, to receive an e-mail, it is necessary to have a modem. Millions of employees do not have access to a desk, let alone to a modem and, thus, no access to the e-mail system. As a method of management communication, it has great merit, although it is still open to abuse. As a means of mass communication, it currently has less relevance, although its capacity to reach more employees is increasing all the time.

Video

A more established and very much lower technology method, is the video which enables employees, and their families, if desirable, to watch in leisure the utterances of a senior manager on a well-made business television programme about the organisation. When it is well done, it can have the benefit of looking like real television, the most powerful mass influencer in the world today. When it is less well done, it can be cringingly embarrassing.

Popular topics are annual results, major mergers or radical new policies because these are issues over which, sometimes, employees have real power and influence. If videos are produced and distributed infrequently and irregularly, which there is evidence to suggest most are, they run the risk of being viewed as being of use mainly as a management tool to try to win over the attitudes of employees on a certain issue. This could, of course, be an entirely accurate interpretation and care needs to be taken that they do not always have a crusading or proselytising approach. One or two relatively innocuous examples can often win more friends than a highly forceful declamation of the organisation's policies on a given topic.

Similar to tape slides, videos do, however, present the best of both worlds. Professionally packaged, they are a serious and sensible piece of communication, which has often been corporately created but which can be locally presented. Introduction notes enable locally based line managers, with whom employees identify, to set the video in its context and enhance the experience of watching it. Packaged question and answer documents also allow the manager to take a wide range of questions afterwards with rather more confidence than he/she might often feel about presenting a corporate viewpoint.

Videos can be, and often are, overdone. There was a rash of the things in the mid-1980s when the technology must have reminded many managers of opening up a new box of toys at Christmas. A legion of video production companies grew up, many of them seriously mediocre and virtually all of them charging outlandish prices to an audience that, initially, didn't know any better. Some of the corporate videos made in the last fifteen years of the 20th century may well go down as among the most gruesome creations in the history of mankind, so crass are they in concept, scripting, filming, production, interviewing, editing and, particularly, sound tracks. For a while, it seemed as though any hard-up student who had once strummed *Hey Jude* on a guitar (with difficulty) could set up as a sound studio and make money. Fortunately, things have improved but many internal videos are still fairly reliant on in-house managers not knowing any better and being seduced by the mystique, language, supposed glamour and eventual dynamic success, real or imagined, of the finished product.

Worse than all that, employees began to grow heartily tired of the wretched things. In one or two organisations, the issuing of a video seemed to become synonymous with yet another plea from management to employees to exert themselves more or to exert themselves in a different direction or to remember to switch off the lights when leaving the loo. This is the kind of feeble content that has effortlessly gained in-house videos their dubious reputation, and helps to explain why they are being created with rather more selectivity than previously. The fact that virtually any feature film and millions of other titles are widely available on professional videos to watch in the home merely serves to underline to the employee the standards which are acceptable and the gulf with those which are not.

In-house Television

Linked to videos and, in some ways, an evolution of them, is internal television. In the right hands, this can be a very sophisticated, albeit expensive, mass communication tool. But, there are snags here too. Vauxhall Motors installed 'Business TV' in its Ellesmere Port plant a few years ago and has taken it out again because it is passive rather than two-way and the employees have quite openly stated that they prefer to be talked to by their own managers face to face.

One of the leaders in this field in the UK, and one of the most successful proponents, is, not surprisingly, BT, with its wealth of relevant technology and advanced communications management. Every two weeks, BT makes its own in-house business television programme called *Vision* for transmission throughout its locations. Some employees have easy access to a desktop monitor set at or near their work stations.

The content is a fairly straight lift from a decent television news magazine programme. Even the current presenter, Deborah Hall, is an ex-television presenter, thus heightening the impression that you are watching a broadcasting service with an element of objectivity which is seeking to present the truth surrounding a number of important issues. Advantages include a more professional presentation package than is always possible by having managers give information face to face and the flexibility of watching. Not only is this not confined to work time, it is not even confined to BT employees. Once that video has gone out, it could end up anywhere. For this reason it always has to be relatively sanitised, which is, perhaps, the only major criticism of it.

Take a typical example, selected at random. One programme has four items (the average in normal circumstances) consisting of:

- the Chief Executive announcing e-mail for all;
- a piece on BT's contribution to the millennium experience;
- BT's global strategy explained;
- why BT is investing £300 million in upgrading its network.

Some of this is clearly of interest to competitors, of whom there is no shortage. Consequently, there is unlikely to be any major revelation in a piece about, say, BT's global strategy. Nonetheless, there has to be enough merit, enough news value and enough new information for most employees to feel that they have had a relatively enriching experience as a result of watching the programme. Another typical programme has a line up of the following:

- Chief Executive, Sir Peter Bonfield, looking forward to the year ahead: a typical senior manager's review of the nation piece.
- A piece congratulating BT engineers on their efforts to keep customers connected during a series of storms and bad weather.
- The outline benefits of the Syncordia solution – highly specialised and not of real interest to outsiders, except the competition.
- An introduction to IT Works, a (then) new initiative launched with Comet.

Here, again, the content could be just a bit too revealing if not treated with care, something that *Vision* does rather well. It manages to walk the tightrope between communicating too much for commercial confidentiality and enough to keep viewers satisfied. Unlike the Vauxhall experience, in which most employees are concentrated in a couple of sites, BT employees are spread all over the country and overseas with very few large concentrations of people.

Packaged Presentations

The packaged presentation (i.e. 35mm slides in a carousel or overhead slides in a sequence plus scripted notes for line managers to deliver) may be old-fashioned technology but still represents a good compromise between remote and immediate communications and one which many managers find less daunting than new technology. The manager is still the person giving the information to the employees, albeit with help. He/she is, therefore, truly interactive with the employees.

The script reduces the chances of unclear commentary, subjective interpretation or human failure in presentation terms and these risks are always present. The slides give a focal point which is visual enough to keep employees' attention for up to seventeen minutes; more than 25 minutes is not recommended, although very few employees presentations seem to weigh in at much less than an hour.

The script also gives the manager a sound prop against which to lean; few managers really enjoy delivering the gospel at arms' length, especially when they may not wholly subscribe to that gospel in the first place. A script at least gives them the corporate alibi and the words can be seen to come from on high rather than from the local manager's office. This can also be a disadvantage in that the commitment of the manager is called into play and his/her sincerity can appear to be less than solid to cynical employees. However, if there is this much cynicism among both line managers and employees in the first place, a packaged presentation is probably not going to be the answer. The big managerial guns probably need to be wheeled out to do the softening up before tape slides given by line managers can be as effective as they should be.

There is a variation on this which is the pulsed tape, a series of 35mm slides linked to a pulsed audio tape which, on arrival at pre-set points in the taped commentary, automatically changes its own slides in the carousel. Again this is now dated technology, but it still works perfectly well and can be preferable to listening to a semi-literate manager mincing the words, sense and language of a script. An added advantage is that the tape can be easily and quickly re-pulsed to add or delete content; this gives the flexibility to tailor presentations to different locations at very short notice. Being low tech, these devices are also less temperamental and somewhat more sedate than more modern technology, such as PowerPoint presentations. These are all very well and good, and very impressive in the right context, but can be tricky to set up, finicky to run and unpredictable in their functioning. They also rely on a human being to change slides at the right time – something which a pulsed tape does not need.

Pulsed tape slides are popular in the more conservative sectors of management, public sector, engineering, SMEs and so on, and there is every reason why they are appropriate for this type of organisation. Even the monitor

can be turned into a projector at the flick of a switch so that a table-top presentation can be swiftly turned into a projected show for a whole room. Quality of vision suffers a little but it can still cope with the average conference
room, which is what most managers want it to do.

Multimedia

Much has been heard recently of this great and, relatively, new phrase, 'multimedia' and sometimes it is talked about as the panacea to all ills, both in
communications and other terms. Maybe, one day, it will be, but, at the moment, it is still being developed and, although many exciting opportunities
are possible, it may be well worth waiting until the technology is more advanced. It may also be worth waiting until managers' understanding of that
technology and what it can and can't do has been developed in parallel.

Clearly, multimedia is already an essential avenue of exploration for many
organisations which are pioneering the development and it promises greater
things, provided the human element is not forgotten. People still want to be
talked to by people, not machines, no matter how glitzy they may be. Moreover, employees usually want to see spending kept within reasonable bounds,
especially at times of possible large redundancies. High profile, high gloss
exotica is, to most employees, synonymous with high cost; cost which, many
believe, could have been invested in jobs and careers rather than in boxes of
tricks. Maybe, therefore, it is better to wait and see on this particular development.

Internal Radio

One interesting internal communications method, which is now almost a backwater, is the internal radio station – ironically, this was seen as the answer to
many problems fifteen to twenty years ago. Now, it is much less popular and
probably becoming even more sidelined as technical advances leave radio
behind. Nevertheless, it can still have its uses, especially in large-scale buildings and complexes. One large engineering group in Glasgow used it to good
effect for several years, although the factories in question were eventually
closed for unrelated reasons. While it was in operation, it proved a useful
tool in two ways. Firstly, it clearly helped to impart information very quickly
and, one hopes, very accurately. That could have been expected.

A more surprising benefit, however, and one which may yet see internal
radio gain a new lease of life, was the psychological impact. Apparently,
music can have a calming influence on humanity. Certainly, experts working
with severely disturbed, and often violent, young people have found that
Mozart is one of the very few ways of exerting on them restraint, concentra-
tion and relative calmness.

Since most of the output of an internal radio station is, inevitably, music, and pretty undemanding music at that, it follows that the calming influence could be significant, although it might be unwise to express it any more strongly than that. Communication bulletins are usually interspersed with a home made disc jockey approach and some of the better and more ambitious organisations have linked up with local radio stations, either BBC or, more often, commercial stations, to relay regular items, such as news bulletins, weather forecasts and traffic reports. This clearly has both an informative and convenience value; in time it can also come to be regarded by employees as a beneficial feature of working for a particular organisation.

Hospital radio has long been a forerunner in this area, although the output is largely for patients rather than staff. However, the format is not dissimilar and is pragmatic enough not to tinker with the proven formulae of easy-listening programmes involving the audience, such as phone-ins and request programmes, and a thin smattering of organisational or local news. More subconscious in its effect than business television and video tapes, it could just be that the internal radio has enough subtle merit to survive for a while yet. It is not, however, an area in which many organisations are investing heavily at the moment.

Most current examples likely to be encountered are in supermarket or hypermarket stores, usually large warehouses where a touch of humanity, such as a human voice, makes a refreshing break from the otherwise tedious outlook of shelves and racking – for both customers and staff.

Hotlines

Open phone hotlines have been used successfully by BT, among others, but are not as widely used elsewhere as they should be. In essence they allow for a phone-in type of service which allows any employee to ring in to talk to a specific manager, usually about a specific topic, at prearranged times. The discussion is not normally broadcast through any other channel, although the transcript of a particularly compelling conversation could always be published subsequently in a house publication.

For the individual employee, however, it is an unrivalled chance to talk directly with a senior manager who has previously perhaps been only a disembodied name, if that. This in itself has the merit of breaking down barriers to understanding. Add to this benefit the fact that, in the vast majority of cases, the employee will leave the conversation thinking more of that manager than he/she did before the phone call – if the manager is any good at all (and if he/she isn't, what are they doing being exposed like this in the first place?) – and the added value of the benefit becomes plain. Hotlines are not expensive, using, as they do, the internal phone system, and, although they might take up senior management time, there can be fewer better uses of this than to secure the commitment of fellow employees.

Intranets

Finally, there are intranets, the internal internet which, when planned and developed with care and forethought can be one of the best possible methods of communicating internally, quickly, accurately and relatively inexpensively. The biggest outlay in terms of effort is to create a network of machines, which are compatible with one another; once this is done and the intranet has been created to fit those machines, there are refreshingly few practical limits to its uses.

Accessing external information is very simple especially when linked into the Internet; circulating it around a global organisation takes a matter of seconds with retrieval as and when convenient. For example, reports on regional, national or international economic trends, trading conditions, political situations and likely financial models can be disseminated throughout the entire organisation within a very short space of time.

It is safe to say that the power of intranets will grow rapidly and, even by the time this book is published, the stage of development at the time of writing will have been exceeded to a significant degree. In addition, internal websites can be made secure from external access and this allows relatively confidential information to be discussed, although, as with any system, the degree of security must always be policed regularly to avoid unpleasant surprises.

The Combined Approach

In truth, the successful approach to internal communications depends not on any one of these technologically based methods but on a combination of several of them as well as on some of the verbal and indirect methods discussed earlier. No single route will be guaranteed to reach the eyes and ears, let alone the minds, of all employees. Only by a judicious combination of written, verbal and electronic methods can the audience be reached, informed and involved.

Take another example from BT, one of the best sources of examples because it is one of the best sources of good practice. When financial results are announced, they are announced internally in a number of ways. There is an internal briefing document, resembling the press release but worded especially for employees. Take the following as an example.

Figure 11.1: BT Third Quarter Results

 *Briefing*

BT's full year results 1997/1998

BT's results for 1997/1998 show continuing strong growth in demand. Although call charges have been reduced by £650 million, BT has improved operating profit. Outside of the UK, BT's presence in Europe is also growing through a number of strategic alliances.

Financial results

- Turnover for the year was £15,640 million, up 4.7% on last year, with overall demand growing by 10%.

- Capital expenditure totalled £3,030 million, an increase of 11.4% over the previous year. This is due to spending on enhancing the network to enable customers to benefit from advanced services and improving the network's capacity for carrying high speed data. Cellnet has continued to expand its digital cellular network.

- Residential lines reduced by only 260,000 despite significant competition, while business connections grew by 360,000 almost all of which were ISDN lines.

- Operating profit increased to £3,657 million for the year. Profit before taxation was £3,219 million. BT paid £1.9 billion in tax this financial year.

- Operating costs grew by 4.7% to £12,355 million. Staff costs rose by an underlying 0.5%.

- BT's European ventures, whilst in an establishment phase, are incurring losses. These accounted for most of the £252 million losses from associates with the largest loss incurred by Viag Interkom which is setting up its fixed and mobile network in Germany.

- There were 124,700 people employed in the business at 31 March 1998, a net reduction of 2,800.

- The final dividend to shareholders will be 11.45 pence per share, giving a total of 19 pence per share in ordinary dividends for the year. The total dividend for the year represents a 6.4% increase on last ear after adjusting for the special dividend paid in September 1997.

- £64 million (2% of pre-tax profit) has been allocatted to the employee share ownership scheme.

A more detailed breakdown of the financial results is on the intranet at
http://swift.boat.bt.co.uk:8080/CRD/HQ/corpinfo/
Issued by: CRD Employee Communications

20 May 1998 *CRD* *xx/98*

That was issued either physically or electronically throughout the company. The salient points were recorded for the BT *Today Newsline* (the phone hotline) while the regular newspaper, *BT Today* ran a more extended version in its subsequent issue. A special item was recorded for the internal business television programme *Vision*. This was released within a few days of the announcement on the following Thursday. A special summary was created for the *BT Today* newscreen which was visible in communal points of assembly such as reception areas, restaurants and some of the larger open plan offices.

The announcement was also placed immediately on the intranet, separate subsections of which are available to varying levels of staff, allowing for differing degrees of detail to be communicated to differing levels of management and interest. And, of course, there was an immediate placement for the release and supporting documentation on the e-mail system. A typical and very illuminating diagram of the processes is shown in the following communications channel diagram.

The BTCRD Employee Communications Channel (see Figure 11.2) adds up to a powerful lot of communication. It all needs co-ordinating, managing, scripting, writing, directing, producing, checking, delivering and assessing. Above all, it needs the will to do so. Without this, there is no *raison d'etre* for any internal communication system, no matter how technologically advanced it may be. There is also always the question of audience acceptability. Arthur Andersen representatives, who are stationed in most countries in the world, are often very heavily dependent on links, such as e-mail, for their contact with the outside world. Here, a recent internal survey, which attracted the quite phenomenal response of 819 replies, showed quite clearly that the technologically based cocktail of communications emanating from central office mainly through e-mail and intranet was not only welcome but invaluable. Eighty per cent of managers who responded viewed the *EFC Broadcast* service as an invaluable link not just with corporate thinking and developments but also, in some cases, with home. Arguably, no other box of tricks can work that magic.

These managers also had strong views in other key areas. Sixty-nine per cent thought the length was right, and 68 per cent read it on the screen while groups voted different sections their favourite, or most interesting parts. Naturally, the internal communications plan was then adapted to meet these requirements, although the adaptation needed was relatively modest.

The mixture of different types of communication method is also well illustrated by Arthur Andersen whose typical plan is set out below. Here nine different types of communication are used to reach all the disparate parts of the organisation, three of them deeply rooted in modern technology. The blend is imaginative and forward looking but practical and not over dependent on electronic media.

Figure 11.2: BT CRD Employee Communications Channel

Figure 11.3: Arthur Andersen Communications Plan

Communication	Outline	Audience	Frequency	Objectives
GCF Broadcast	Electronic bulletin covering up to the minute news and items and a message from JAT.	All GCF employees CMPs AA Leadership	Monthly	• Profile JAT/Leadership • Promote successes • Immediate feedback • Easy access to major news
GCF Exchange	Magazine style communication with AA/GCF news and future plans	All GCF employees CMPs AA Leadership	6 monthly	• Informing and entertaining • Motivating and uniting • Profile leadership • Highlight successes • Strengthen the culture
GCF Announcements/Cutt ings	Electronic bulletin AA/GCF important happenings and appearances in the press	Select groups	Ad hoc	• Communicate key announcements • Promote successes • Easy access t o major news
Global Partners Conference	1½ day meeting	GCF Partners and Managers	Annual	• Involvement in strategy • Profile Leadership • Communicate policy and goals • Networking
Regional Conferences	2 day meeting	GCF Partners and Managers	Annual	• Involvement in strategy • Profile leadership • Communicate policy and goals • Networking
GCF Wins Communication	Quarterly edition of GCF Broadcast to focus on Global 1000 and major wins	All GCF employees All AA Partners	Quarterly	• Raise profile of GCF amongst all AA partners • Highlight successes
Internal Promotions	Promote GCF across other service lines at their conference, e.g. ABA employees video *Risky Business* or internal trade fairs	Select groups	Ad hoc	• Increase awareness of GCF across the firm
Knowledge Space	GCF area on intranet available WW to every employee affords exciting communication possibilities and interaction	All GCF employees All AA partners	Ongoing	• Immediate access to major news • Global information sharing across all of GCF and AA
Induction Pack	Outline information on GCF in a folder which can contain all the above to provide an introduction to GCF	New joiners to GCF Members of AA (non-GCF)	Ad hoc	• Promote AA • Promote achievements and opportunities • Enhance sense of belonging to a global firm

CHAPTER TWELVE

The Indirect Approach

Ethics

It may be that an organisation doesn't always want to communicate directly with its employees. Sometimes employees may be overly suspicious of their employer's motives and stance, they may not welcome an approach from management; in some cases, they may simply not know who management is. For whatever reason, there are occasions, and they occur more frequently than the public may think, when the management of an organisation wishes to harness third party communication in order to get over to employees a point of view which they otherwise might not accept.

The ethics of this can be dubious and much depends on individual circumstances and point of view. The end result has to be important enough for an organisation to run the risk of alienating influential third parties, such as the press, and to have its corporate reputation besmirched if it is discovered – because that is what is quite likely to happen. If the risk is worth running, there are some unofficial rules, but the objectives of the exercise must be really worth the candle in order to justify the risks of an indirect approach. Also, it must be almost impossible for practical, logistic or political reasons to attempt this type of communication in any other way if the indirect approach is to be justified.

Practical Applications

Take a typical example. An organisation is about to enter its annual round of pay bargaining, possibly anticipating difficulty in getting X,000 employees to accept a rise at or below the level of inflation. At around 2-3 per cent, that's not surprising; nobody really likes to think that they are losing out in the salary stakes. So, that organisation has to prepare the pitch. It has to start to shake the confidence of the employees and their negotiators about the assumption of a rosy future for everyone; it has to start to destabilise complacency and disturb any inherited belief in the security of job tenure. It has to talk about uncertainties in the future. These may be all too real, or they may be the product of a fevered, but creative, imagination. Either way, the last thing the employees will take direct from the management is a threat to future employment in advance of a pay negotiation; that appears too much like blackmail, which may not be an unfair interpretation.

Moreover, the employees are not likely to believe this fairly transparent ruse, at least not twice. If the circumstances are right, it can be achieved once by direct communication, but more than once is pushing it to the extremes of employees' belief. So, another way has to be found to shake the certainty of the bargainers, to get over unpalatable messages about job security, overall costs, inefficiency and the logical consequences of possible site closures and redundancies. If the employees are not going to believe this if it is contained in a message directly to them from management, in what form are they going to believe it?

Media

The answer, very often, is through the press or broadcast media. Surprising though it might seem, most people believe what they read in the papers and what they hear on radio or see on television. Unlike a direct management approach, they believe that the journalist or broadcaster has researched the story, weighed it in the balance and is presenting an objective account, impartially written and presented and that the resulting piece of journalism is relatively truthful. In any case, since management has not directly communicated anything contradicting this version to the employees, they have very little option but to believe what is in the papers.

So, the carefully 'leaked' rumour comes into being. Never attributed to anyone at any time, but, perhaps, the result of a shady 'source' inside the organisation, the leaked rumour is a lethally effective weapon in the right hands. In the wrong ones, it is a self-destructing cruise missile without a control system.

In our mythical example, the communications or PR function in close consultation with the other senior managers, will draw up a report containing a strategic review of some kind, recommending the closure of certain sites and the redundancy of most employees at those sites, unless certain economies can be made in operating costs. Uncannily enough, those savings often equate roughly to the total cost of that portion of the pay rise, which is at dispute in the forthcoming negotiations.

The existence of this report, which may well exist in practice and may be absolutely genuine, is then leaked to a carefully chosen journalist. It is not enough to choose any old journalist, it has to be a writer with credibility and standing in most of the circles in which the pay negotiations will take place. Thus it probably has to be a national paper, unless the organisation is restricted to one or two locations.

In the UK there are currently eleven national papers to choose from and countless television and radio news magazine programmes. The type of organisation dictates the choice of paper; suffice to say that, the middle of the road papers (the *Daily Mail* and the *Daily Express*) are quite popular for this kind of tactic because they appeal to more than the employee; they appeal to the employee's family and these are the two titles most heavily read by women.

Equally, if it's mass appeal an organisation needs, nearly half the literate population of the UK read *The Sun*, *The Star* or *The Mirror* between them every day, while local radio is one of the main influencers of local opinion.

In a traditional, predominantly male organisation, which is where a lot of strikes take place (railways, engineering and manufacturing for example) the strikers' weak link is often the family. If employees' wives, who have to find the money for the weekly supermarket shopping, are unsure about the future of their husbands' jobs, their moral and practical support for any form of industrial action may be greatly reduced. This is especially so in the case of a strike with the misery of low strike pay which may have to be endured for some considerable time. There is evidence to suggest that many strikes have been averted by this type of ruse and that the impact of many others has been markedly lessened.

So, the journalist and the newspaper are selected, and the story is unaccountably leaked. Nobody ever admits to this; often the very existence of such a strategy paper is denied for some time, to help maintain its credibility. But the insidious work has been put into practice. The poison, in true Iago fashion, is doing its work well. Uncertainty doesn't so much creep into the employees' negotiators' psyche as hit them between the eyes – or the shoulder blades, depending on your point of view. From that point on, the management view is more likely to prevail. If the employees' representatives back down, the settlement will often be around the figure which management wanted in the first place. The strategy paper may mysteriously be allowed to lapse, or to lie dormant until such time as it is needed again – perhaps in real life the next time.

If the employee negotiators do not back down, the management has a ready-made base from which to appeal over the heads of the negotiators to employees and their families. Management can describe the existence of what has become a very legitimate strategy document and point out that future jobs cannot be safeguarded if any industrial action takes place. To most employees and their families, to customers, investors and the public, it sounds reasonable and credible; it is a licence to cut jobs, sites and functions until the books balance, or until something better comes along, such as a merger or takeover.

In point of fact, of course, many of these strategy documents really do exist and have been worked up by business planners, not for the convenience of a propaganda campaign, but for the possibility of corporate life becoming too difficult to maintain at its current level. Often, they really are classified information and very few people outside a boardroom, or a senior management committee, know of their existence, let alone their contents. They have a role to play and it is not a fictitious one.

Equally often, organisations do not really want to reveal the existence of such documents because that may start speculation among competitors, customers, investors, government and all the other stakeholders and observers about the viability of the organisation, whether it be in the public or private sector. Strategic plans are, after all, a vital part of most organisations' thinking and a simple way of approaching emergency planning. They were not created to beat the employees over the head, but, if the need arises, they are better than a knobkerrie.

Ethics in Practice

There are two big problems with all this: the ethical one and the practical one. Is it right to use what, often, can amount to dubious methods to provoke acceptance of a package, or a broader message, which may not be as generous as the organisation can really afford? Equally, is it right to use or exploit a relatively innocent third party, such as a newspaper, to achieve this end? Readers will draw their own conclusions.

The practical issues are more tangible and can be even more daunting. What happens if the journalist finds out that he/she is being duped? Journalists are not noted for their complicity in the machinations of large organisations, especially those in which public sector money is at stake, which may be the case. Those journalists who feel they have been professionally used and abused are likely to turn on their tormentors and rend a good deal of flesh; more to the point, they are likely to do it publicly – and that can be disastrous for the corporate reputation of the organisation concerned.

To continue the hypothetical example. If the *Daily Mail* or the *Daily Express*, or any other newspaper or radio station, finds out about the strategy document from a trusted source, they clearly wonder why the information is being leaked. The leak puts them in an invidious position. If they print the story, it could be construed that they are abetting a fairly shabby, although not illegal trick and they lay themselves open to public accusation of being corporate or government lackeys – not a traditional journalist posture. If they do not follow up the leak and use the information, they are missing out on a potentially massive story which could scoop the headlines and reveal the true and shaky state of one of the nation's largest or most important or most newsworthy organisations – and no news editor likes to turn up the opportunity to do that. So, what does the news editor do, apart from wish that he/she was on holiday and that it is somebody else's decision?

This position is even worse if the strategy document is a fabrication, and this approach is definitely not recommended. Whatever is contained in this strategy document genuinely needs to have at least a kernel of truth, otherwise it can too easily be discredited. Journalists are too shrewd to accept such a gift at face value, and so is the news editor. They will seek to find out what lies behind the scoop by asking around, and herein lies the other part of the problems of trying to use the indirect method.

Wherever the journalist investigation turns, the story must be corroborated. So, industry observer, watchdogs, senior civil servants, whatever third party sources and observers the journalist will approach, have to be primed in advance. Either they are persuaded to collude, which is not unknown, or they must already have been given intelligence that the strategy paper really does exist and that its contents may really be as dramatic as the journalist suspects. Then a quiet phone call, an 'off the record briefing' and a discreet drink in an anonymous pub, and the cat is successfully out of the bag.

This, then, is the other main strand of indirect communication, the need to influence the third party opinion formers outside the press and media. They have a standing as impartial authorities to whom many observers and stakeholders, including employees and journalists, may turn for advice. At the very least, they are likely to be listened to when they utter words of wisdom about the organisation concerned, or even the industry sector to which it belongs.

Events in BMW/Rover in early 1999, for instance, yet again showed the importance of the automotive industry panjandrums in academia whose opinion is counted very highly by all involved – management, unions, employees, investors, politicians and general public alike. There is a handful of academics, several of whom appear on television or are quoted in the press when crucial decisions on the future of what's left of the British motor industry are in the balance. Professor Garrol Rhys of Cardiff University is one eminent and very knowledgeable example; Professor Khris Bhatacharia of Warwick University is another and there are others, less well known, who are not backward in coming forward when asked by the media to provide an expert opinion.

Positive Briefings

Clearly, it behoves the organisation about which these experts are expected to comment to ensure that such impartial observers and experts are briefed as fully and as positively as possible. This is particularly true for the message which management wishes to get over to a host of audiences, including all those mentioned in the last paragraph. Foremost among these audiences are the employees and their families who, ultimately, may have to take the decision, yet again, about whether there is a future for Rover or whether it might just as well be shut down in advance of bankruptcy. The management line could be very simple. If employees were to vote for a strike, there is probably no future at all; if they accept major improvements in working practices, higher productivity levels, some (more) redundancies and relatively pegged pay, there may be some sort of future. Sadly, this is exactly the point at which this book started, and the company in question has hardly moved on in the intervening twenty-odd years. The issues now are almost identical and the outcome will probably be, predictably, just as depressing.

Political Observers

Another favourite source of this type of indirect communication is the political world. If academia is not slow to be interviewed during a series of focal
issues, neither are politicians of all shapes, sizes, political complexions and
levels of importance – or self-importance. All organisations' locations exist
within a parliamentary constituency, for instance; therefore there is always
an MP whose role can range from the detached to the almost embarrassingly
involved. It is well worth ensuring that these politicians know what is going
on, why and what they can do to help. Some of their influence may be needed
with influencers, such as government, investors, analysts and customers.
Equally, these influencers may be of direct relevance and great interest to the
employees, some of whom may know the MP and many of whom may have
voted for him/her.

So, here is another strand in the indirect approach – briefing expert political and influential opinion to help to colour the tone taken by the press and
media which, in turn, will help to colour the opinions of the employees. It
can become rather involved, but it can be made to work very effectively.
Larger organisations usually have a cogent public affairs policy designed
partly to keep key public figures of all sorts abreast of developments, trends,
needs and other key issues. Sometimes these include internal relations; often
they don't. Yet an MP's statement or question in the House can be a very
effective way of underlining the management point of view. If uncontrolled,
it can also be a very effective way of torpedoing the management point of
view.

However, MPs are not stupid and they may be reluctant to be drawn into
a situation that looks suspiciously like washing dirty domestic linen in public. So, rather than briefing them once the need is palpable, the art is to keep
them briefed on a continuous, if low key, basis. Only then will they really
believe that the organisation understands the MP's need for information and
may respond accordingly. Some of them never will, but others, usually the
majority, can be understanding and sympathetic. As with many forms of enlightened PR, it pays to make friends before they are needed.

The briefing does not need to be elaborate. A quiet lunch once a quarter,
even a beer in a convenient pub will often suffice. MPs are busy people and
do not want to have their time wasted, but they do want to know about major
issues in areas such as employment, job creation and job loss, which may
affect their chances at the next election, or may enable them to make a rapid
name for themselves in the House.

Those who surround MPs are, paradoxically, often rather less helpful but
even keener to get in on the act. Private secretaries and research assistants
have it in their power to make organisations' life a lot easier or a lot harder
and it sometimes seems as though their stance on this is so arbitrary that it
depends on which side they got out of bed that morning. Many political ad-

visers are privately despised for this type of behaviour while being publicly fêted in the belief, erroneous or otherwise, that they are highly influential people, that this is the kind of intelligence service they want and that it will ultimately benefit the organisation to provide it.

It is almost always easier and cleaner, therefore, to deal directly with MPs wherever possible. They themselves will sometimes prefer this too but individuals vary wildly, depending on factors such as their seniority and their diaries. Clearly, it is difficult to set up regular briefings with the Prime Minister or senior cabinet ministers, although it has been known to happen. Certainly politicians' private secretaries have very stressful lives, often having to organise the MP's entire waking moments, whether political, business, family or social. However, an approach from a senior figure in a major organisation often works rather better than one from a relatively humble PR person, especially if the senior figure has a reputation in public life. Here is one really useful role for the chairman-like figure and one in which most good chairmen excel.

Local Politics

Politicians do not stop at MPs. Many of the local politicians are also only too keen to jump on a publicity bandwagon, especially if they can make a local name for themselves. Self-aggrandisement has never been far from many public figures. They also exert a pressure on employees, indeed, some employees may well be local councillors, school governors or non-executive members of public sector bodies. Consequently, there is a double need here, which is to keep the local politicians off the back of the organisation while still influencing them to influence the employees in what is perceived to be the right direction.

This is not an easy task and can involve more kowtowing than most senior managers care to undergo. At the very least it takes a few lunches with the right people in the right, and usually most expensive, restaurants. But the rewards can be worth it, although probably less so than for the efforts to influence MPs. It can often be a damage limitation exercise and there may be a case to make some kind of gesture – perhaps sponsoring a civic event, supporting the mayor's charity or providing some help in kind to an, apparently, impoverished local authority.

The ethics of all this are highly dubious but that has not altered the facts for centuries and is unlikely to do so for considerably longer. Care has to be taken not to become enmeshed in the maelstrom of local government politics, which can be both petty and nasty. Cases such as the Poulson, Alderman Cunningham and T Dan Smith unholy triangle on Tyneside which came to light in the early-1970s are not that isolated and it is likely that very few of them ever emerge in public. Self-respecting organisations are not keen to be involved in and implicated by one of the exceptions.

A cardinal rule is to stop short of anything that could reasonably be interpreted as bribery, either to an individual, a political party or a local government authority. To give them their due, most public sector authorities are pretty good about this; even bottles of wine at Christmas are discouraged. Unfortunately, we are talking here about something more insidious than a bottle of Maçon Rouge – the problem is more often the type of pressurising which gave rise to the UK's Nolan committee of inquiry into standards in public life, standards which are gradually being brought into some kind of ethical line. That line will never be shell proof, but it can present a more cohesive face of respectability than has always been the case in recent years.

Parochial Politics

There is also a lower level of local government, which it is unwise to ignore. On the basis that the small details are often the largest problems, most communications managers will have on their list of potential irritants a number of these bodies, especially town and parish councils. Although neither of these tiers of local government actually wields any true power, there are occasions (such as planning applications) when they can influence decisions made by larger bodies, such as county, district and borough councils, and their sense of civic pride is undiminished, even sometimes inflated, by their relative size.

For the purposes of internal communication, these bodies have a very real presence in the public arena. Sometimes, employees or their partners may well be elected members of such a body and this can give them a double view of an issue, which affects the organisation and the community alike. A planning application, for example, although often not in the direct control of either a town or parish council, will usually be referred to one or the other by the local planning authority. Similarly, an issue regarding aspects of the organisation which directly affect the life of the local community, such as traffic, parking, noise, pollution, effluent or other environmental concerns, crèches, employment and redundancy and local sponsorship, are issues which can be affected by the employees themselves – because most of them are members of that community. It follows therefore, that the community in which they live can also colour employees' views on their employing organisation.

Consequently a number of more enlightened organisations have worked out that employee and community relations are two sides of the same coin. Unfortunately, many more have not yet made this link and the exigencies of global recession may force some to regard this conjoined strategy as a relatively minor consideration. It is not. In fact, the good will of both employees and communities may make the difference between survival and extinction for some organisations during the first two decades of the 21st century.

At the risk of using a BT example again, that company has around 8,000 employees who are also members of local councils, school governors or who serve in some other voluntary and relatively prominent community work.

The overlap between what they are told and what they wish the community to know about their organisation is clear and huge. They cannot represent BT as a leading player in its field and a caring and socially responsible organisation if they are not, themselves, convinced that it is, indeed, worthy of this label.

Community Relations

BT may be unusually large, but it is also typical of the overlap in worlds (the working world and the community and leisure world, which surrounds home life), the understanding of which is essential to any serious practitioner of internal communications. How a community thinks about a neighbouring organisation is quite likely to colour the thinking of many of that organisation's employees because they are an integral part of that community.

Consequently, the whole area of community relations takes on a different guise when viewed in this light. A local sponsorship for a socially worthwhile project becomes even more important; it might just make the difference between employees regarding the organisation as money grabbing and mean and their thinking of it as a reasonably civilised outfit with its heart in the right place. So, all the plethora of small, local community sponsorships and support activities are often important to the internal communications manager.

The scope for these sponsorships is endless; hospitals, nursing homes, hospices, medical research and care causes and related charities are currently among the favourites, certainly in the UK where there is now an awareness that the state cannot afford to pay for everything. Often, the sums involved are relatively low, sometimes in the hundreds rather than the thousands and this represents real value for money in internal communications terms as well as community terms – provided employees know that the support has been given, to whom and why. Then they are likely to be more supportive of their employer and to think of it with some degree of moral ownership. Clearly, attitudes will not change overnight but they may become less hardened and more receptive, which, in terms of the internal objectives, is all that an exercise of this nature is intended to achieve.

The types of community sponsorship and support can vary greatly. Anything to do with health is currently perceived as being a good idea; education also, but this is a more thorny path. Often the connection between the organisation and the education body or cause has to be justified before the help is warmly received. Often it may never be received warmly at all, since education seems to have more than its share of world weary cynics. There was even an instance, in 1998, of a British education authority refusing to accept a gift of books from a major supermarket chain on the basis of some specious but politically correct argument which sought, in vain, to prove the gesture patronising and socially divisive, in the process perhaps attempting to conceal the likelihood that the teachers were out of step with public opinion. Ironically, the supermarket received much good and positive media coverage for this churlish refusal in a way which can hardly have been planned and which allowed it to emerge smelling of roses by comparison with the graceless refuser.

Despite this, anything to do with children is usually a sure-fire winner and not only because many employees may have children. Children's issues are emotive, their welfare a matter for all and their chances in life not limited to circumstances of birth. Any help which organisations can give in broadening education, including the type of education in preparation for life which is either not taught in schools or is taught only indifferently, can be very well received among many sections of the community. Not only does it make good media copy, it also helps to make good employee attitude.

Children Power

There is great scope for helping children in many ways. Those who are disadvantaged in some way are perhaps the easiest to help through schemes of social 'enabling' and introducing to aspects of society that would otherwise remain closed. Even 'normal' children can always benefit from scholarships, aid in sport, recreation and education, special holidays, shadowing or work experience and a host of other services which may not make a great deal of financial difference to the organisation but which can enlighten children's lives beyond all expectation. The reward of seeing this occur is enough is itself but a further reward often lies in the improved attitude towards the organisation very often undertaken by those employees involved or made aware of the circumstances.

For example, NatWest employees benefit from a scheme by which the company matches pound for pound everything the employees raise for a children's home in Crawley. This gives a double incentive – the good which can be done by their own money and the knowledge of the additional benefit of the other 100 per cent which will be contributed by their employers. In 1997, the NatWest Employee in the Community Award saw 3,813 staff receiving community action awards for the specific voluntary action with which they were associated. These include causes such as rape and sexual abuse centres, Citizen's Advice Bureaux, over 1,700 educational activities, National Debtline, the Local Investment Fund for Community Enterprises, Royal Shakespeare Company tours, Forum for the Future, children with brain damage and Save the Children, a typical range of good causes.

Further, NatWest employees raised over £1.5 million for charities, such as the McMillan Cancer Relief Fund, in their local communities during the same year. A further £4.3 million was contributed to special investment in which help through either cash, kind or staff enterprise and expertise was allocated to local causes. It's a classic win-win situation and everyone ends up with a benefit of some kind.

Similarly, The Body Shop encourages its employees to take off every Friday afternoon – on full pay – to help with a local community initiative, usually in education, health or the voluntary sector. Self-worth is raised among employees as is a feeling of respect in their employer, another win-win situation.

Nestlé supports causes, such as the Salvation Army hostels for the homeless, the Medical Research Council, Employee Volunteer Award scheme, which gives each employee up to £1,500 to spend with local community volunteer groups and the Special Helper Award which awards up to £10,000 for employee-nominated causes, such as the Byker Bridge Housing Association providing housing for the homeless or the Lidgett Grove school's aromatherapy centre for disabled children.

Children's homes, children in care or need, those abandoned or afflicted, are all deserving of assistance in some way, even though the state may provide for their basic needs. To put this into practice as part of an enlightened employee and community relations policy is not only helping the practical alleviation of distress, it is also sound business sense.

Voluntary foundations and charities, too, sometimes benefit from this fusion of corporate reputation policy and philanthropy, but extreme care is needed in these cases. Relatively few of these deserving causes are often very concerned about the reputation of the organisation that is helping them; they have their own priorities and often a very difficult financial balancing act to manage. Consequently, they are not likely to have the resources to trumpet news of this help to the skies and, as a result, employees and public alike are often kept in the dark about the true facts and the generosity and approach of their employer.

Also, there is an argument which says that capital should not be made out of other people's distress or disadvantage for the purposes of marketing or corporate reputation, and internal communications can sometimes be viewed in this guise. There is a sound ethical principle here which is not very flexible and with which it is best not to tamper. Exploitation is perceived as distasteful, shallow and exploitative, and that cannot be good for any organisation's image, either internally or externally. So, think twice before launching into a programme that will use this type of mechanism to raise profile; often something less contentious and more applicable can be found.

There is, for instance, the GAYE type of scheme (Give As You Earn) which is similar to that of NatWest. In it employees opt for a percentage of their salary to be donated at source to a designated charity, usually drawn from a short list approved by the organisation. The employer then matches the contribution pound for pound in a way similar to the NatWest example. This is another way of binding in the attitudes and actions of the employee to that of the organisation and another way of trying to reach the same consensus of opinion on social issues, which is halfway towards influencing that employee when it comes to a hard decision.

Press and media do not always have to be used as an unwilling mouth-piece. Sometimes, employees' activities are newsworthy in their own right and gain coverage that, while never spectacular, can be useful for internal perceptions. Almost anything that involves employee participation is a good story, provided the participation is legal, well intentioned and benefits a good cause. Self-indulgent pranks are not recommended, as the charity worker who did a topless bungee jump soon discovered. If the story was worth writing up, why did she have to take off her top? If it wasn't a good story, what was the charity doing trying to hoodwink the press into believing that it was?

But fund raising has its place in both the employee activity and the local media. So do a number of community works which have been supported by the employer, although they must be non-political and non-contentious. Happily, they are sometimes remembered by stakeholders when times are harder for the organisation and this can bring its own dividends.

Influencing the Family

Another example of the indirect communicating method is letters from management to employees at their homes, already touched on from a practical point of view in Chapter 9. Usually the signatory has to be a very senior person and the issue a major one in order to justify the exercise. Here the appeal or message goes straight to the employee's family, thus cutting out the immediate possibility of too much filtration by that employee which could bowdlerise the message. On the other hand, letters to homes are an intrusion; working life coming into the home unbidden is not popular in the UK, particularly among those who are employed, as opposed to the self-employed, who have very little choice.

Consequently, it can backfire. Families may resent it as much as the employee and that will have the exact opposite effect to the one that was intended. For this reason it is usually reserved for issues of extreme urgency, such as future site closures or a massive relocation. As a result, the letter looks as though it's going to bring bad news even as it lands on the hall mat, and that can be a damaging handicap.

Home and family life is at such a premium in an increasingly frenetic and neurotic world that any intrusion from a place of work is likely to be unwelcome for many employees and their families. To influence the major influencers on the household, the message must first of all be important to that influencer. Very seldom is this the case except in dire circumstances, such as financial disaster, strikes or potential closure. By that time, the damage may already have been done, but the letter might militate against harsher feelings. In practical terms however, it is unlikely to be much help.

An extension of this, which is logical but clumsy, is to send a lot more material to employees' homes on the basis that the family should have the right to see everything which affects the employee. While this may be enlightened in motive, it is usually misguided in practice. Not only does it increase the intrusion into private space of the employee, it can also be wasteful and reduce the impact and credibility of any specific communications addressed to the home. An occasional bulletin to keep families informed of key issues and organisational progress may be valid in certain circumstances, however, it can be overdone and anything above three or four pieces of communication a year is likely to be the top limit for most practical purposes.

There are occasions, however, when this type of exercise can be used to good effect, usually in helping to prepare the way for a clearer understanding of critical events or developments within an organisation, perhaps a merger, takeover, closure or relocation. Since these events don't happen very often, they are justified in having their own dedicated communication process.

Other ways of getting at employees indirectly include running promotions at local supermarkets or other centres of retail business, which are likely to be frequented by employees and their families. Here, in the relative relaxation of the weekly shopping, the message can come across as being subliminal and may last longer in the employees' mind, and that of the family, than it would otherwise have done. Special offers for employees of given organisations at given outlets are nothing new – the civil service has been doing it for decades – but packaging these as enhanced internal communication and making sure that employees realise their existence and value is a more recent step.

Employee Events

Special employee events, either with or without families, are as old as most organisations. Their success varies greatly depending on the type of character the employee may be. Some are born gregarious and enjoy the occasion; many are not and do not. However, the theory goes that a day out at the races, on a Channel ferry, at a west-end show or in a Greek restaurant is as attractive today as the famed charabanc works' outings of former decades. Whether they are to everyone's taste or not, and they usually never please everyone, they can have a binding effect on employees, even if only to unite them in horror at the artificiality of the contrivances to which managers resort. Sometimes, the sheer ghastliness of it all follows a close second.

An extension of this thinking is the Open Day, when families can inspect the organisation's premises and see the work on which their family representative spends so many hard days. These efforts are very time consuming and gruelling in their organisational and administerial demands. If the organisation is of a reasonable size, it will almost certainly need the attentions of a full-time post for at least six months prior to the event.

They can, however be very successful. The Austin works at Longbridge (long since renamed many other things but still always referred to as 'The

Austin' by everyone in south Birmingham) were thrown open to employees'
families in 1981 when the then new Metro was launched on the back of all
the glittering new robots. This was a great success and helped to create a
rather better atmosphere than had been the case for at least eight or nine
years. At the time, the plant employed around 17,000; around 35,000 people
visited the plant in the course of a single weekend. Successive cuts in the
workforce unfortunately eroded much of the good work, but this was not the
fault of those who organised the open days. Many other events on a smaller
scale can work equally well, provided the organisation is honest and allows
open access to most areas, with the exception only of those sections out of
bounds for safety or commercially sensitive issues. Employees and their families are usually united in wanting the organisation to be honest and open.

Rumour Mongering

As a generalisation, employees are usually relatively apathetic en masse; only
a small vociferous minority ever regularly voices strong opinions. Where
these opinions can be influenced or neutralised, employees will often be reasonably committed. There is a supposedly new technique for tackling this
aspect which was unveiled with great pride at a public meeting on internal
communications a couple of years ago – the concept of peer group influencing. In effect, this entails identifying the rumour mongers in any given section of the organisation and subtly feeding them titbits with which to influence their fellow employees. Needless to say, it was announced with a certain amount of smugness by a woman from a consultancy who, presumably,
was safe in the knowledge that if it all went pear shaped, she wasn't actually
working in the direct line of fire and could always pick up another unsuspecting client if things got really difficult.

If she may be believed, it was her practice to feed bits of gossip, some but
not all of it of an internal political nature, to a few blabbermouths and then
watch it run round the organisation. In her, possibly, mistaken belief, this
constituted internal communications. Since she worked for one of the larger
and better known consultancies specialising in this area, it is interesting to
imagine how many notable clients have fallen into this trap and how many
innocent employees and their families have been caused anxiety and hurt as
a result of this callous type of manipulation. Unhappily, there are no safeguards worth the name over most PR and internal communications consultancies, no matter how stridently the industry proclaims that there are, and
this practice is probably still being sold, at a high price, to several unsuspecting client organisations.

Crass though it might sound, it undoubtedly happens and the announcers
of it even sounded proud of themselves. Maybe it has a place in some
Ruritanian romance or in a small backward state buried in some forgotten
jungle. It is difficult to accept that it needs to be employed in a modern, well-

managed organisation, which is committed to a modicum of internal communication practices. There were rumours that Moshe Dayan used it to good effect in Israel in the 1960s, seeding rumours of Arab incursions, atrocities and threats and thereby raising the determination of the Israeli armed forces to resist defeat. That, however, was a singular case of highly dangerous real politick in a highly volatile world. Anyway, nobody could ever find out for certain whether the rumours were rooted in any truth. It would be nice to think that most modern organisations do not have to share those pressures or those methods, although it's always possible that they do.

As with the leaked strategy document, if rumour mongering is to work it has to be done very cleverly, far more cleverly than those who announced it appeared to be treating it. For a start it must be very sparing in its choice of titbit, timing, rumour monger, leaking method and monitoring system. If just one of those elements is not in absolute harmony with the others, the whole scheme could backfire like a 15th century cannon and with far more lethal effect to the gunners. Any internal communications function resorting to that regularly would have to be pretty desperate.

There are occasions when this kind of game can be relatively harmless like setting a hare running and seeing what happens. A colleague derives innocent pleasure from starting jokes, anecdotes or stories at three-day workshops and seeing how long it takes for someone else to tell him the joke in the bar. That is innocent fun, especially if the joke is a good one in the first place. But the cynical manipulation of the gullibility of many employees is not a step to be recommended unless there is absolutely no option. If there isn't, it may be too late for this method to work in any case. If an organisation can communicate with itself properly, there is no need for this drivel. If it can't, it needs professional assistance, not quackery and specious manipulation.

Trade Unions

At one time, trade unions used to be fairly dubious themselves in some of their methods but seem to have adopted a lower profile lately. Falling membership may have something to do with this as may a series of disastrous disputes in the early-1980s, culminating in the miners' strike of 1983–1984 in which management, to quote *The Sunday Times*, "plucked defeat from the jaws of victory" on a number of occasions, ostensibly to break the power of the hard-line unionists once and for all.

How permanent this 'solution' will turn out to be is another matter. In the infancy of a new millennium, militancy is by no means dead and buried and ominous rumblings about planned industrial disputes are once again being heard in several key sectors such as transport, education, health and manufacturing. Nevertheless, unions need to redefine their role in light of modern developments. Seen by many as latter day dinosaurs desperately trying to pretend that they are as relevant now as they were in the late-19th century, the future of trade unions is highly doubtful, especially as their own political party appears to have forsaken so many of the sacred cows of trade union doctrine which it once observed.

It may be that, with the increase in non-union organisations, the trade union simply fades away. Its job of defending the rights of workers, whoever they may be, has largely been achieved. The challenge now will be to find something remotely resembling full employment in the developed world, rather than worrying about the odd differential dispute in which pride is likely to be all that is at stake. But pride has a stubborn way of surviving even the most logical onslaught and, it would be a brave and foolhardy observer who would write-off the militant unions just yet.

Clearly, there needs to be clear and open communication with unions, just like any other employees, but not with any sense of priority or the privilege with which they have so often cloaked themselves in the past. The responsibility for managing remains with management, not with trade unions; Thatcherism achieved that, if nothing else. They are kept informed out of courtesy rather than need. The sight of management reasserting itself is a healthy one compared with the crippling prevarications of the 1970s and early-1980s. A large part of this assertion is the process of internal communication, in which the unions bear no direct role or responsibility.

As an indirect audience, trade unions have not, traditionally, been among the most useful. However, faced with common issues, such as economic downturn, ever-developing technology, successive waves of overseas competition and a raft of social problems, it may be that a new era of management/union co-operation could dawn to try to create a united front with which to meet some of these issues.

While unions may, or may not, still have an influence over various aspects of internal communications, indirect audiences are very much with us for the foreseeable future. The only successful approach is, of necessity, subtle, difficult, delicate and sometimes devious. It requires a high degree of strategic thinking, a fair measure of good fortune and a whole-hearted commitment to the communities in which the organisation operates. But it is a very high risk area of activity, best used as a last resort and, even then, only if there is a particularly effective practitioner to drive it through. If in doubt, leave well alone.

CHAPTER THIRTEEN

Into the Future

So, as we come to the end of a survey on internal communications, there are one or two loose ends to be tidied up. One concerns the use of the once current, but now fading, terminology that describes an aspect of internal communications as internal marketing.

Internal Marketing

'Internal marketing' is a good marketing ploy for a few consultancies and contains the germ of a decent idea. It is, nevertheless, an outworn term, relying as it does on the premise that everybody in an organisation spends most of their time busily marketing their services to everybody else. That's the sort of process that systems people used to employ in the 1970s and quality people in the 1980s. Eventually, the systems and the quality were near perfect, but often the organisation was producing nothing and servicing nobody. Consequently, bankruptcy beckoned more quickly than the spurious certificates which were the sole reward for these modish but unsustainable ideas.

Interestingly, the champions of this school of thought (notably Kevin Thomson in his book *Corporate Internal Marketing* published by Pitman in 1990), take as a starting point the fusion of marketing and HR. Great, what happened to communications? Yet the need for strong and professional internal communication runs through Thomson's entire book, despite the fact that it is never directly addressed. Thomson even acknowledges that internal communications is an essential component of internal marketing, but then leaves the topic alone. How anyone can purport to be creating a new pinnacle of internal communications without actually talking about the topic is a matter for conjecture and might rival a Sherlock Holmes plot for contrivance, intrigue and mystery.

There is, however, some recognition that the shift of responsibility for internal communications, without mentioning the term, should move from HR to marketing. Back in 1990, Thomson seemed to be thinking more globally than many of his peers, perhaps hoping to create a new movement, a new management philosophy for the extension of his idea to world organisations. Perhaps this is why it conveniently overlooks the issues of internal communications and the skills, issues and problems involved on the ground.

For these reasons, and because it is still being hawked around as an idea a decade and more after this book was published, internal marketing may turn out to be a flash in the pan, a Thatcherite backwater with little lasting credibility. It may just, however, turn out to be a way of making responsible internal communications more appealing and more relevant to more managers, and if it achieves even a tiny fraction of the work which needs to be done in this field, many practitioners will be grateful to Thomson for some time to come.

The other main problem with internal marketing is that its concepts are not in the realms of the thinking for most non-profit making organisations where marketing as a concept is not fully developed, if it exists at all. Thomson assumes a marketing function and role for his organisations – with reason. However, when canvassed for her opinion on internal marketing, an internal communications manager in a major local authority asked whether it included team briefings, if it didn't, she didn't want to know. That type of approach may be a hurdle which is simply too steep to overthrow within the reasonable future.

For these reasons, Thomson's ideas about internal marketing are probably too complex and too ambitious for many of the players in internal communications. At the same time, they have something to offer as an idea and may well be worth a glance as an indication of an approach which is more ambitious and more Thatcherite than conventional internal communications and is aimed at large, complex and essentially highly commercial organisations. It's probably too complicated for small and medium-sized organisations and the entire spectrum of the public and public related sector. But times may change and a version or a development of it may have a role to play at some stage in the future. How and whether it can blend harmoniously with more modern developments, such as intranets, is another issue altogether.

Internal Customers

The internal marketing school of thought is, however, based on a sound principle, that of the internal customer. The theory goes that most people in any given organisation serve customers either externally or internally and that they themselves receive a service as a customer from others within that organisation. The external kinds of customer are obvious: those who pay for the goods or services offered by the organisation; in the case of the public sector organisation, those rate and tax payers who are the customer.

But the internal customer takes a bit more believing. The closely linked theory is that every job in an organisation has some impact or other on customer service in the external world because the jobs all support each other. So, a salesman relies on the production department, which relies on the purchasing department, which relies on the engineering department, which relies on the research and development department, which relies on the business planning department, which relies on the finance department which relies on – who? The salesmen, or the shareholders or board.

It is a moot point whether shareholders may be customers. They are certainly stakeholders, but the whole thing is getting more than a bit tenuous at this juncture. Many shareholders would rather that the organisation simply got on with the job of keeping the external paying customers happy.

However, it is possible for some employees in many organisations to draw up a basic flow chart of all those people who provide them with some sort of internal service and also those to whom they provide some sort of internal service. Having done this, the wisdom goes that the employee asks whether it is possible and/or desirable to make changes to whatever he/she does to improve the effectiveness of this two-way service. In many cases, it will certainly be possible, but whether it will be desirable or politically acceptable is another matter.

For example, it is usually relatively easy to spot scope for improvements in the areas of reliability, speed of response to requests, depth of service in terms of detail, prioritising, comprehensive service, realistic promises, intelligible communications and so on. However, to admit that all these areas have been done less than perfectly, or even inadequately, for some time requires a certain selflessness, which is not frequently found among most human beings. Of course, there is scope for change – there is also scope for change in the way we live – but that doesn't mean we are going to carry out that change. If we were to do so, we could eradicate most military and civil strife, crime, disease, racial and gender inequality overnight. That seems a pretty far-fetched point of view; and the internal customer principle is really a microcosm of that scenario.

Minor changes may be acceptable to some. The deep and innate conservatism of most human beings with a lifestyle that keeps them out of the poverty trap is, however, an overbearing enemy to this nice sounding but not too practical theory. On paper it looks fine, but then so did Marxism 100 years ago.

The Academic Management View

There are some management tomes around which heap praise on the internal customer concept as though it had just been discovered. Some of what they say is sensible and well thought through; some is not. There is one school of thought that, again, must remain anonymous, which refers to a six-point memorandum for developing strong internal customer service through internal communication. While not remotely contentious, it isn't very deep either.

The six rules are:

1. **Keep staff informed** because that will keep them more satisfied and less likely to be mushrooms.

2. **Money is not everything in life**, short-term gains in staff efficiency are

all that can be expected from monetary incentives. Job fulfilment is a more certain method of achieving a long-term efficiency.

3. **Career progression** is one of those ways of achieving that efficiency, especially when linked with clear goals in internal customer service and overall strategy.

4. **Getting staff involved** in the process and responsibility of work is another area of motivation in that employees will feel more attuned to the organisation's objectives and culture.

5. **Praising** is not something that comes easily to many managers, yet is one of the most powerful tools in the staff commitment battle.

6. **Communicate to staff**, only the sixth in the pecking order of rules but at least the author got there in the end.

This is typical of many modern schools of management as it is being taught in universities, management schools and colleges. As with many other types of training, there are very variable levels of competence in this approach; some of this training is very good, but much of it is pretty mediocre. The drive towards NVQs will no doubt begin to have a standardising effect at some stage (and IIP is doing so already), but this is a slow process and will not bear fruit for another decade or so.

Furthermore, standardising is all very well when standards are being improved; when they are being degraded, it is not so helpful. Only the most blinkered observer would really pretend that a nation can create over 50 universities in a few years and expect standards to remain as high as they were. For a start, where are the qualified lecturers coming from? And what were they doing before these universities were created? Also, internal communications is a rather practical proposition for many academic tastes and, to be taught properly, requires a depth of experience at the coal-face, which is not visibly or widely found very often among academic staff.

Information Flow

Perhaps key to the whole internal customer process is marshalling the information flow to staff. We have looked at this fairly extensively earlier in the book but a summarised flow chart might help to bring together a number of the threads which illuminate the whole approach to internal customers, which is in essence a parallel with internal communications. A typical virtuous circle flow chart is given below.

Figure 13.1: The Virtuous Circle of Communications

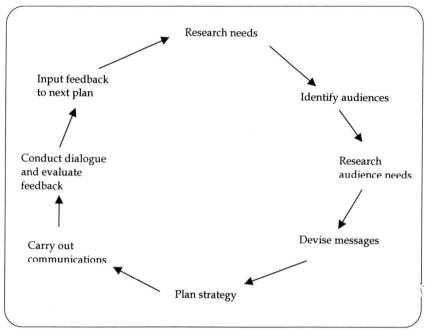

This eight stage process should see most organisations through most eventualities.

NIH

One of the most insidious obstacles to the smooth running of this or any other internal communications process however, is the pernicious NIH factor. Standing for 'Not Invented Here', this is a particularly dog in the manger attitude all too prevalent among managers at all levels. The theory runs along the lines of ' . . . any initiative or anything that has been dreamt up by another person or department cannot have any value because I didn't think of it first. Furthermore, since it could affect my function, my peers may question why I didn't think of it first, therefore, I'd better do everything I can to discredit it and prevent it being accepted or put into operation'.

This is a difficult one to combat if the opponent to the initiative is a senior manager, as can often be the case. The more senior the manager, the more he/she has to lose and, thus the more grudging he/she can become, especially in the public or service sectors where innovation is often not exactly welcome. When positions become entrenched and future job security and pension entitlements threatened, there is little point in relying on logical arguments to try to resolve the intractability. Logic has nothing to do with emotive thinking, fear, apprehension, jealousy and ambition are all much stronger motivators.

In a serious case of senior level NIH, the only successful course of action in the long run may be to remove the blockage altogether. Usually this will already have occurred to other senior managers, partly as a result of the behaviour which often accompanies NIH, such as petulance, sulkiness, refusal to co-operate and deliberate filibustering to slow down or derail progress. However, severance can be expensive and very difficult to push through in the face of determined opposition, so promotion out of harm's way to a relatively tranquil pasture for the remaining years of contract can often be a cheaper and less confrontational option.

Most readers will know of instances of this; some may have wondered why the step was necessary and NIH may well be one of the key factors. Never was utilitarianism so clearly demonstrated as in subjugating the individual interest to that of the general good of the organisation as putting out to pasture a manager who may have given his/her all but who may now be disinclined to embrace new thinking, new processes, new strategies and new people. No amount of internal communication effort can ever really redress this particular dilemma.

Feelgood

As a factor and a force in modern management, NIH is linked to the feelgood factor. More familiar to many, this is the state in which a sense of security, usually false, is allowed to infiltrate most management layers and starts to dictate terms of policy and strategic thinking. A close relative is the 'Porsche Syndrome'; when starting up a new business, some entrepreneurs go for the best material object as a first purchase with all that capital which the bank has injected (usually a Porsche or equivalent) and worry about nicer details like cash flow and order books afterwards. It was more common in the 1980s than it is today, but the feelgood melody lingers on. Look at the number of BMWs on a motorway; it would be interesting to ascertain how many of them are owned outright and how many leased. Further, how many of those leased are being driven by a really useful employee in a really viable organisation? There is no way of knowing for sure, but lease repossessions are not exactly decreasing.

Feelgood is seen in one of its most dangerous forms in internal communications. Here, a sense of well being born of apparent employee commitment is one thing – complacent but maybe not terminally so. When a feelgood assumption masks employee fear, ignorance, apathy or disquiet however, it is entirely different and can lead to such an air of unreal complacency and unworldly unreality that it can quickly lead to a deteriorating organisation.

Modern information technology is one of the major areas in which feelgood can operate. As we have seen, just because the technology exists to talk to people in Katmandu every day doesn't mean that managers should do so, or that those in Katmandu can return the compliment, or that either the home office or the Katmandu office really understand what is being communicated, never mind whether they agree with it or not.

Communication of any kind needs to involve an effort, otherwise it might as well not happen, just as sending Christmas presents requires an effort of some sort or else it might as well not happen either. Only an effort to do the following can the effort be said to have been made with genuine willingness:

- discover what is needed;

- design an appropriate communications programme;

- put it openly and honestly into practice; and

- follow up and ascertain reactions which are incorporated into feedback for the next phase of communications planning.

Otherwise, it is simply a question of the nearest and easiest Christmas present being made to do because it's too much effort to go and look for the right one for that particular person.

Where Next?

So, where exactly is internal communications going over the next decade? Where will it be by 2010 and how will it be carried out?

Answers to this type of question are sometimes temptingly easy to dream up and, just as with Christmas presents, their value varies in relation to the amount of effort put into the answer. However, here are a few of the more likely scenarios as provided by some of the people in the profession who should know what they are talking about.

First, there will undoubtedly be more technology upon which to call for help in communicating internally efficiently. As a colleague remarked recently: "By the time your book is published, all the technology will be out of date" – he could be right, which is another reason why this book does not major on technology. If you want answers to technological questions, please see a computer systems expert.

As a layman, it is safe to say, however, that the capacity to draw upon enriched e-mail, intranet, video conferencing and other indispensable forms of communication will be enlarged greatly over the next few years. This will be a 'good thing' provided it is treated like fire – a good servant and a bad master. We have seen elsewhere in this book that too much technology can be used as a blind, a barrier and a shield behind which to hide. No amount of electronic boxes can replace eyeball to eyeball communication.

A recent example published by *The Sunday Times* bears out the point:

> A motorist, following the satellite-guided navigation system in his car, drove past a stop sign, down a ferry ramp and into the

river Havel in Eastern Germany. A police spokesman said, 'That sort of thing can happen when people rely too much on technology.'

Second, the global dimension will also increase rapidly even for organisations that do not currently have many overseas links. Increasingly, they will have such connections, or they may not have a business. Even small companies, which would have been viewed as parochial a few years ago, are now cultivating markets, suppliers and partners in a number of countries and the electronic revolution has encouraged this by allowing easy access to contacts thousands of miles away.

This has consequences for internal communications, especially when organisations are represented in many different countries. While the principles remain largely the same, indeed they can be extended since the further away an office is geographically, the further away it is ideologically as well, the logistics need to be taken into account.

One obvious area is language. Many regions in the world are happy to accept English as the business language, but an increasing number are not. While we have to thank British and US economic imperialism over the last 250 years for the very wide acceptance of English, there is a growing influence that would like to see it replaced. Fortunately, for those of us whose first language is English, the exact language with which to replace it is one of the topics on which its detractors cannot yet agree: Chinese, Russian and Arabic are regularly touted, with the first of these becoming the most likely candidate in the long run (if only because of the sheer volume of people and business involved). In the past, there have equally strong challenges from French, German and Spanish, most of them now marginalised for practical purposes.

Many large multinationals have their chosen in-house language, which eases the situation a bit. However, even this might not always find favour in other territories. Just try communicating to a French subsidiary in English or German and see what, if anything, happens as a result. Where the situation is unclear, or where there are overseas operators who cannot be expected to have a good enough working knowledge of English, it is only common sense as well as courtesy to have it all translated. This has many pitfalls, but willingness to oblige is not one of them.

The pitfalls include occasions when the translation is not acceptable to the overseas office, perhaps on a technicality or in its style. While this is a fair comment if the translation is indeed faulty, it can often mask NIH in the shape of an unwillingness to accept that there is an overseas master in the form of a controlling company. One pan-European organisation which spent a great deal of time, effort and money getting its in-house newsletter right for all markets found that the German office was perennially complaining about the standard of translation. It offered to let the German office translate the material itself, but the office didn't have time. It offered to let the office vet the translation, but the office didn't have time. It changed translators twice but still the complaints kept coming. Finally, in despair, it stopped the newsletter going to Germany altogether – and promptly received complaints that the Germans were being left out.

If Malaysia was seen as a win-win situation, Germany was seen in this instance as a lose-lose situation. In the end, the organisation stopped the newsletter altogether and simply let the Germans moan. This is not peculiar to Germany, which is usually rather more enlightened in its management attitude, France, Belgium and Italy do their share of whinging as well. In Europe, only in Scandinavia and Holland is a willingness to work in English really expected and accepted.

Elsewhere, the Middle East expects to see its communications in Arabic, and, while Singapore, Malaysia, Hong Kong, the Philippines and, to a lesser extent, other parts of South East Asia are content to work in English, Chinese is a rapidly growing force. Eastern Europe and the Balkans are embracing German as well as, inevitably, Russian while Central and South America have long been Spanish speaking US hegemonies. The real emerging force may turn out to be the African continent where English is almost the only uniting factor and where economic growth, slow though it may be at the moment, will eventually have its day.

Against this patchwork quilt of a global internal communications forum, each individual organisation has to come to terms with its own international culture. Some, US and French companies, for instance, often insist on English or French being used respectively; others are less dogmatic and more pragmatic to the needs of individual nations. It's a case of deciding which is best for the employees, and, ultimately, the customers, of the organisation in that country. As such, it is a decision best formed with the help of enlightened input from the countries concerned rather than being imposed centrally from above.

Time is another aspect to be taken into account, although the advent of electronic communication has rendered this less of a hurdle than it used to be. Still, it is a good idea to remember time differences especially when carrying out a delicate communications exercise. Clearly, something released in Singapore or Hong Kong at dawn (their time) can easily be loaded on to the electronic jungle telegraph and beat any conventional attempt to communicate the same message at dawn in London or New York. So, preventive action is necessary to ensure that all employees receive the same message at the same time in their respective countries. The international finance markets are quite used to dealing with this kind of situation so workable patterns for coping do exist.

Cultural differences, too, and an organisation's sensitivity to them, can dictate the success or otherwise of an international internal communications campaign. Arab sensitivities, especially with regard to Islam, have been a potent factor for many years (at least since the 1973 oil crisis) and continue to overshadow much of the dialogue between the West and the Middle East. Less stridently proclaimed, but equally sensitive, are issues of culture in the Far East and South East Asia where good manners still prevail amid a more tolerant climate, for the moment, than exists in the Middle East. In either region, there is not much point in attempting to impose a major strategy without prior consultation.

In South East Asia, too, Islam is a growing factor, although the recent difficulties in both Indonesia and Malaysia may retard its progress, especially among the emerging middle classes. More important, however, and increasingly so, is the emergence of the Chinese influence with its emphasis on negotiation, win-win strategies, the need to maintain face and dignity and the prevalence of tactical exchanges of power. The 'Chinese Box', in which an opponent is always left with a way out, is a prevalent force in dealing with the Orient; so is the interpretation of time, which can be very elastic, cultural sensitivities and due respect for elders and betters.

Little things which are easy to overlook in the UK, Europe or the US mean a great deal more in the rest of the world, and it behoves any organisation either to engage local national staff to advise on this and massage all internal communications accordingly or else to steep themselves in the country's culture as much as possible. In any case, this latter step is common sense; only a few brands as powerful as McDonald's and Coca Cola are strong enough to survive the vagaries of the world's cultures. In the crystal ball, there is little evidence of nationalism for successful enterprises, although it will continue to be a nuisance even for those organisations, and every indication that all these cultural differences will have to be treated with rather more respect by many Western organisations with ambitions to become world players, let alone world leaders. The really successful multinationals, such as Nestlé, worked this out some time ago and are geared up to cope. Many others are not.

Complex Structures

Thirdly, internal communications will become more complex. In many organisations there is no longer a conventional hierarchical structure in which management communicates easily to the workforce, which hears and obeys. If it ever was like that, it isn't any more. There is a very blurred demarcation line between management and staff; everyone wants to be a manager, which, at least is a refreshing change from the 1980s when everyone wanted to be a consultant. Staff are graded but have different opinions of their grades, stations and responsibilities and this is an increasing trend. Flatter structures, with more people in the middle and fewer at what used to be called the bottom, are now the prevailing direction in many new types of organisation, especially those in the IT world. The pyramid is rapidly becoming a diamond.

Complexity in organisations, often fuelled by increased management training and a series of bewildered management layers, can make internal communications even harder than they were before. Management theory is fine but it often is just that – theory. Do organisations really put into practice Belbin, McGregor or Maslow when they return from a management workshop? Do they really go round mentally giving each other hats or role models? Some may, but others may be too busy getting on with the task of running the business.

Leadership

Fourth is the cult of the individual who is a strong communicator with his/her staff – and, rightly, this will not go away. One manager in a retail and distribution company is still remembered for his team communications and leadership twenty years after his retirement. His characteristic memos (known as Gilligrams after his surname) are still affectionately hoarded in dusty desk drawers and his time at the helm is viewed through rose-tinted spectacles because he took the trouble, time and effort to communicate professionally with his staff.

One development, which will help internal communications, is the increasing weight being given to motivation. Motivation is no longer regarded as money or existence – although it was only in 1992 that Buchanan and Preston recorded an English foreman in an engineering plant as saying:

> People only come to work for money. You're not telling me that if you just left them they wouldn't go and have a chat or sit down and read the newspaper. If you're telling me that wouldn't happen, then one of us is kidding – and it isn't me.

Despite that, motivation is becoming a much finer art and one which cannot be achieved without a strong level of internal communications on both a personal and a group sense. Although this book is specifically not about personal relationships at work but about the corporate need to communicate within itself, there are aspects of motivation which can enhance that process.

Figure 13.2: Maslow's Hierarchy of Needs in the Form of a Pyramid

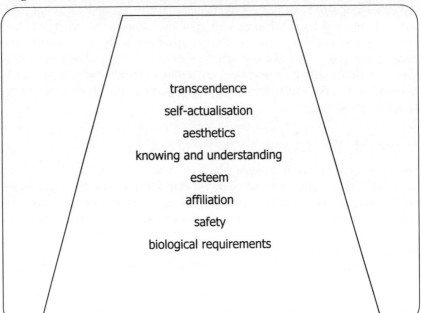

transcendence

self-actualisation

aesthetics

knowing and understanding

esteem

affiliation

safety

biological requirements

Maslow's 'needs' are now legendary in management training. But how does internal communication fit into them? Several of the needs assume good communications as a basis – affiliation, esteem, knowledge and understanding and self-actualisation in particular. But there is a ninth need which is much less frequently seen in management courses: the freedom of enquiry and expression, a need which is a prerequisite of all the others.

This cannot be achieved without professional internal communication. A climate has to be created in which the freedom to enquire is implicit; how else can one find out about working circumstances of any kind unless by enquiring? It is when this freedom to enquire is deliberately balked that intransigence and disruption begin, as in disputes based on the right of management to inspect and publish findings in, say, teaching. Accountability, public in this case, cannot be achieved if access to information is denied; this is the slippery slope of totalitarianism in which a self-perpetuating elite relies on the continuance of a professional mystique in order to justify a relatively cosy existence. Clear communication, outwardly as well as inwardly, is sometimes the only way by which this dragon can be slain.

Overall, internal communications is a push/pull process (being pushed by managers and pulled by employees) where it works properly. Sometimes both managers and employees need incentives to carry out their end of the process especially if other matters appear more pressing, which can be most of the time. When it works well, however, internal communications can be a self-sustaining process, which emanates from an almost hidden function, so subtle and unobtrusively efficient are its workings.

Internal communication is also likely to become more instantaneous, partly as a result of all the new technology, partly because employees can now find out elsewhere the truth about an issue long before management has decided to admit to it. In such circumstances, management has little choice but to fit in to the overall scheme, which means 'communicate and be damned'. This is going to mean faster thinkers, faster reactors and faster operators, another reason for taking the practice out of the HR area and putting it somewhere where managers are habitually used to reacting quickly. Only if HR changes, as it is showing signs of doing, to embrace new thinking, new techniques and new willingness to improve skills as a continuous process (such as the IPD post experience course at the University of Brighton, which has some excellent HR practitioners) are we going to see it preserved as a mouthpiece for communication. Even then, it is likely that this responsibility will increasingly be shared with a broader communications role – PR, corporate communications or even marketing.

All this is likely to make managers take the practice of internal communications more seriously, and that can't be a bad thing. If it becomes seen as the aid to corporate survival, which it is, and as an inextricable component of a will to win despite whatever else is going on, the winners are going to be both employers and employees. But, before this can happen, it needs to be accepted as a grown-up management science, which, when taken seriously can significantly improve the health of the organisation.

Moreover, there has to be, and the signs are that there may be, an acceptance that striving for good internal communications is a bit like trying to find the Holy Grail. It is a quest that is unlikely to be fulfilled in anyone's career because, as soon as real progress is made in one area, it will usually be discovered that remedial action is needed in another. No matter how good internal communications are they can always be better.

We all have a Grail within our organisations, only through our employees can we begin to attain it.

Index